GROWING OUT

About the Author

Barbara Blake Hannah is a Jamaican author, journalist, film-maker and cultural consultant. She trained as a journalist, then emigrated to London and worked as a PR executive for the Jamaica Tourist Board and government. She became the first Black TV journalist in the UK in 1968, starring in TV programmes *Today with Eamonn Andrews* and *ATV Today*, and working as a producer on BBC TV's *Man Alive*.

In 1972 Blake Hannah returned to Jamaica as a PR officer for the first Jamaican film *The Harder They Come*, and continued writing articles and books, becoming a Rastafari and articulate campaigner for acceptance of the religion. In 1984 she was appointed an Independent Opposition Senator, the first Rastafari to sit in the Jamaican Parliament. In 2001, she served as a member of the Jamaican delegation to the UN World Conference Against Racism (WCAR) in Durban, South Africa, where she was appointed a member of the special plenary on reparations, after which she established the Jamaica Reparations Movement that led to the establishment of the government's Parliamentary Commission on Reparations (2008). She presently serves as Cultural Liaison to the Jamaican Minister of Culture, Gender, Entertainment and Sport, and continues to work in the film industry.

GROWING OUT

Black Hair and Black Pride in the Swinging Sixties

Barbara Blake Hannah

With a new introduction by
Bernardine Evaristo

PENGUIN BOOKS

PENGUIN BOOKS

UK | USA | Canada | Ireland | Australia
India | New Zealand | South Africa

Penguin Books is part of the Penguin Random House group of companies
whose addresses can be found at global.penguinrandomhouse.com.

First published by Jamaica Media Productions Ltd 2016
First published with a new introduction by Penguin Books 2022

001

Set in 11.6/15pt Fournier MT Std
Typeset by Jouve (UK), Milton Keynes
Printed and bound in Great Britain by Clays Ltd, Elcograf S.p.A.

The authorized representative in the EEA is Penguin Random House Ireland,
Morrison Chambers, 32 Nassau Street, Dublin D02 YH68

A CIP catalogue record for this book is available from the British Library

ISBN: 978-0-241-99376-7

www.greenpenguin.co.uk

Livicated to Amy Jacques Garvey

Publisher's Note

In this book are some expressions and depictions of prejudices that were commonplace at the time it was written. We are printing them in the book as it was originally published because to make changes would be the same as pretending these prejudices never existed, and that the author didn't experience them.

Introduction

For many people the 'Swinging Sixties' was a myth predicated solely on the charmed young rock stars, artists, actors, errant debutants and models who sashayed down the King's Road and Carnaby Street, and made headlines with their wild antics. Or at least that's what I thought until I read Barbara Blake Hannah's memoir, *Growing Out: Black Hair and Black Pride in the Swinging Sixties*, a gorgeously exuberant account of her decade living it up in London as a young woman.

A middle-class journalist back home in Jamaica, when the opportunity arose for her to travel to England as part of a film in which she'd been given a minor role, she jumped at it. Single, confident, carefree and ambitious, she was soon moving in aristocratic and artistic circles, among people who wanted to change the world. The young creatives of her acquaintance probably had no idea what the future held for them: the Australian Germaine Greer soon became Britain's leading feminist writer; Richard Eyre would one day become the Director of the Royal National Theatre; and the film-makers James Ivory and Ismail Merchant were then at the start of their legendary Merchant Ivory Productions.

Parties, politics, nightclubs, restaurants, concerts, films, openings – Blake Hannah made sure she was at the centre of the happening scene, aware of her exotic status as a black woman and the fashionable kudos she conferred on her white suitors when she walked into rooms draped on their arms. Living in rented accommodation, sometimes sharing, sometimes on her own, she spent many years ensconced in a garret right in the heart of London's West End.

While Blake Hannah couldn't avoid the pervasive discrimination faced by people of colour, including an awful strip-search as soon as she landed from Jamaica, it's interesting to read about her disconnect from the majority of Caribbean people who, at that time, struggling to make their way in the not very maternal 'Motherland', were far too preoccupied with cultural adjustment and survival to be swept up in the waves of a cultural revolution. When she first encounters the run-down city districts like Ladbroke Grove, where most of them lived, she describes their 'loose, threadbare suits, heads covered by narrow-brimmed hats, feet shod in broken-down shoes – all wearing an air of suffering or sadness, of total dejection'. The class and lifestyle divide is never more apparent and her gaze on her fellow immigrants makes stark the difference between the now well-recorded Windrush era narrative of struggle and her own rather more glamorous sojourn as a girl about town.

Blake Hannah is clearly beautiful, and we get a strong sense of her lively and engaged personality. Her conversational writing tone feels as natural and vivacious as if she were sitting opposite you chatting. Through a high-society friend she found secretarial and eventually other white-collar jobs, and she wrote features for major publications such as the *Sunday Times* and *Cosmopolitan*, before, amazingly, becoming Britain's first black television journalist at the ripe old age of twenty-five.

When Thames Television recruited Blake Hannah as a reporter for their early evening news and magazine programme, headed by Eamonn Andrews, who went on to become a famous figure in British broadcasting, her appointment made the papers and turned her into a celebrity, but it also rankled with the outraged racists who crawled out of their slimy sewer pipes and wrote ceaseless letters of complaint to her bosses. Nonetheless, for a brief period she was sent on assignments nationwide, interviewing among others Prime Minister Harold Wilson and the actor Michael Caine, but a mere nine months in her bosses shamefully bowed to pressure and she lost her job. A second television gig ended in the same way.

Blake Hannah writes about this past with stoicism, but reading about her experiences reminds us how hard it was for her generation to make their way all those years ago when raw racism – bottom-up, top-down – was such a barrier to achievement. We can trace the paucity of representation of marginalized communities in so many fields today back to these earlier roots of systemic discrimination. This talented young woman who was bright, personable, aspirational, capable and willing could have had a long career in television, perhaps ascending to the heights of top commissioning and directorial positions, but instead her career was crudely, heartlessly and unjustly chopped off at the knees.

She returned to Jamaica, where she joined the Rastafarian religion and communities, a spiritual homecoming she describes as a wonderful 're-birth, the start of a new life in a Jamaica I had never known before, never even knew existed'. This set her on course for a very different and ultimately more fulfilling future, building up a career as a film-maker, arts curator, consultant and the writer of many books, and she made history as the only Rasta to ever sit in the Jamaican Parliament, doing so as a non-political independent.

Growing Out as a title is symbolic of the journey the author undertook during this period of her life. Black women and hair is an important pairing addressing cultural affirmation, symbolism, self, social acceptance and bias. The author's own hair journey begins with the straightened curls of her youth, with their close approximation to whiteness, and progresses through to the long dreadlocks of her religion, tied up in a headwrap according to its conventions.

Memoir holds an important role in literature as a medium through which we transmit real life stories that cannot be dismissed as fiction. This one is a record of a black woman's journey through a Britain of half a century ago, at once unique because of the career she carved out for herself, but also unfortunately familiar because of the obstacles facing her.

Memoirs by women of colour in Britain are still quite rare, and *Growing Out* enriches our literary history while being a fascinating and hugely enjoyable read.

Bernardine Evaristo
August 2021

Prologue, 2021

There was a place in Jamaica called 'Heaven' where some of my good friends used to live. It was not a place many people could visit – the people who lived in Heaven were very choosy about who they allowed to go there.

Heaven was a colony of shacks on the hillside of Wareika, the notorious haven of criminals and the poor, where Rastafari bloomed after its escape from the razing of the West Kingston 'Dungle', or dung hill, where they had made their humble homes.

Heaven was the place the police continually busted open when they raided looking for ganja and criminals.

Heaven was a place with the most beautiful view of Kingston Harbour.

If they caught an intruder in Heaven, the residents would sometimes strip them naked and force them to walk back down the rocky pathways to 'civilization' on the main Windward Road, facing public embarrassment. But if you were a welcome guest in Heaven, you could sit and smoke a fragrant spliff and listen to the long-time residents and elders of Rastafari discuss life, the world and the greatness of God, JAH RASTAFARI.

The 'criminals' of Heaven were what one friend of mine called 'the rebel slaves of an unjust society' – men whose alternative to starvation was robbery and violence. Crime was the only means of livelihood for those who found themselves adults and near-adults in a society in which they were not equipped to earn a living, except as manual labourers – an occupation with greater supply than demand in the Jamaican ex-slave colony.

The 'criminals' of Heaven could be identified by the sweet harmonies they produced when gathered around a guitar in a hymn of praise to Zion – harmonies perfected in the many years of confinement in the Hell of the General Penitentiary, Kingston, where they served lengthy and unjust sentences for the 'crime' of smoking, possessing and selling the Holy Wisdom Herb, or for releasing their anger and frustrations in acts of robbery or violence.

It was in Heaven that I first learned about the equality of man, the possibility of a world in which each received according to their needs, gave according to their ability and lived in love with their fellow men and women. The residents of Heaven called this philosophy 'COMMUNAL-ism' and said it came from Africa.

On moonlit nights when the shacks and houses of Heaven's hillside were clearly outlined, the residents would be lulled to sleep by the rhythms and harmonies of Nyabinghi Rastafari singing and drumming coming from the yards nearby. In the peace and love which filled the entire hillside community, men hiding in the hills from police arrest would creep gently down through the macca bushes and gather in the dark of mango trees to add their sweet harmonic voices to the concert of praise to the Creator, JAH.

Heaven! What sweet memories!

Chapter One, 1964

You know, you can't imagine something you haven't experienced. I had a picture of England which was generated by the film of the coronation of Elizabeth II, which they drove us over from Hampton, the posh boarding school in St Elizabeth, to see at the nearest cinema in Mandeville, forty miles away. We had on our best school uniforms and those of us who had Union Jacks waved them, and the English girls attending our school whose parents lived and worked in Mandeville's bauxite industry just sat and looked smug.

Another powerful image of England came from Enid Blyton's *Nature Lover's Book*, which I had read in detail, all about beech trees and lichen and sea anemones. I knew all about Trooping the Colour, and tea.

I saw England as a magic land into which I would just arrive and suddenly no longer be the awkward, unattractive beanpole I was, but a svelte, vivacious, beautiful, much-wanted woman, hugging my knees à la Audrey Hepburn in *Breakfast at Tiffany's*, living life to a background music of a lone trumpet playing in the summer evening twilight – you remember that scene in *Jazz on a Summer's Day*, don't you?

Movies really blow your mind, you know. All my experience of the world was based on books, and then when I understood about movies, I used to go to them not only to live out the fantasy for two hours, but to work up new fantasies for myself. Carib was the nicest Kingston cinema. It used to have a sweet smell as soon as you got to the ticket desk.

Usually I would go on Saturday afternoons, which was when all of us teenagers dressed up in our best clothes and hoped that the boy we were currently in love with would come and sit beside us after the lights went out and put their arms around us. That was a big demonstration of commitment and kissing was as far as we girls let the boys go. It was called 'necking' and you couldn't neck unless you were sitting in the back row. Only the very brazen girls sat alone in the back row waiting for their boyfriends and kissing. We 'good girls' sat in the middle rows.

Smoking cigarettes was the big 'bad thing' to do. Sometimes you would beg a cigarette from the boy and try not to cough too loudly on the first puff. But although I wanted to be normal and have a boy come and sit beside me, I was really more interested in the movie. Once the picture started I would watch and listen to everything. I didn't like Westerns unless the hero was good-looking, like Tab Hunter or Richard Egan or Fernando Lamas. He was married to Esther Williams, the swimming star, who was my heroine.

Once I wrote to Fernando Lamas for a photo and he sent me an autographed one. It took me a long time to realize that the signature was printed, and not written by hand. I wrote to Debbie Reynolds and Eddie Fisher too, when they were the Favourite Couple. They each sent me a picture.

One of the movies I loved in my teenage years was *Carousel*. My sister and I went to see it one night at the Tropical, an open-air theatre, and we had to walk back home because we stayed to see the beginning again and all the buses had stopped running, but we walked home singing the songs. My sister sang really well. She could harmonize, but I always learned the words quickest. We were always singing together. I would think of myself as a sexy Eartha Kitt type, but my sister would laugh at me. She used to swap me her supper for pictures of Grace Kelly and she cried the night we saw *High Society*, because Grace had married her Prince and that was her last movie.

I liked *Imitation of Life*, the Lana Turner movie about the White Black girl whose mother was Lana Turner's Black maid and she didn't want to acknowledge her, and I cried when Mahalia Jackson sang at the maid's funeral at the end, because I was glad that the poor Black woman got such a nice funeral. Remember that stupid movie?

I loved Pat Boone. I went to see *Friendly Persuasion* because he sang the theme song, which I liked but didn't understand what the words meant, which meant that it must have been about love and how you felt when you were in love. Anyway, I went and fell in love with Tony Perkins and swapped my sister my supper shortly after that for a photo of Tony Perkins jumping up on a diving board, which she found in a movie magazine. I liked *Stalag 17* because Daddy took us once when we were young and he laughed and laughed and laughed out loud at the part where they had a rat race and the rat that was winning suddenly went mad and started chasing his tail. We were embarrassed and said, 'Daddy shush,' but he used to take us to see that movie every time it came round again and laugh just as loudly every time the part came on that he liked.

I liked *Porgy and Bess* because the Black people in it seemed like normal people, not the maids and slaves they usually played, and the singing was good. And I LOVED *Jazz on a Summer's Day* and *Black Orpheus*, which I saw on a double bill the night I got out of hospital after measles/bronchitis/gastroenteritis. Both of these films made me feel like the person I wanted to be. Marpessa Dawn, the heroine of *Black Orpheus*, was the Black woman I wished I could look like.

But I guess what really made me want to go to England was the fact that films had amply prepared me to exist in and appreciate Europe's cities and lifestyle. Films, and music.

'Rock and roll is here to stay'.

There was nothing to contradict the truth of that statement in Kingston, Jamaica, in 1964. On WINZ from Miami, Florida, Jamaicans listened through heavy static to the popular lyrics of the musical era which gave youth its freedom and attitudes. Ears glued to radio sets each night, we became familiar with the songs of Elvis Presley, Bill Haley and the Comets, Pat Boone, Bobby Darin, and the Platters.

Jamaica still basked in the glow of 'Independence' – a great word, a feeling, a political reality. It had been two years since the start of Independence, and the memory was still fresh of a ball-gowned Princess Margaret gazing sweetly up into the eyes of a tuxedoed Prime Minister Alexander Bustamante in the waltz which marked the official beginning of it all. Still fresh too, in our memories, were the ceremonies, fairs, shows, extravaganzas, speeches and promises which marked 'Independence': the opening of the Sheraton Kingston, the first hotel to be part-owned by the Jamaican government and a foreign hotel chain; the opening of the Esso Oil Refinery, with its sky-high, ever-burning flame rising over the slums of the Dungle; the start of a brand-new holiday – Independence Day – to replace Emancipation Day, which we were told was a bad reminder of our slavery past.

'Independence' held out the promise of a magic wand with which we could make our national fortune, a Jamaica in which we would become instant heroes and heroines. The land would become prosperous and give forth the kind of plenty that we were accustomed to seeing in American films and magazines. As if to prove this correct, Independence had brought us our first cotton candy machine and our first Miss World – honey-skinned, honey-haired Carol Joan Crawford.

Bliss.

So it did not seem in the least bit incongruous for young Jamaicans like me to be memorizing, singing and dancing to the words of 'A White Sport Coat and a Pink Carnation' or 'Silhouettes' or 'Dream Lover'. We were simply in training for the time when we would take our place in that fantasy world defined and described by Fats Domino, Johnnie Ray, Jimmy Darren and The Big Bopper.

'Blueberry Hill'.

'Let's Twist Again'.

'This Magic Moment'.

'Diana'.

'Dre-ee-ee-ee-eam'.

Somewhere below Cross Roads, where the 'lower classes' sported, Jamaicans were making a new music called ska, the beginnings of reggae. Above Cross Roads, the crowd at the popular 'Glass Bucket' nightclub existed in blissful ignorance of this trend, or if they indulged, did so conscious of the fact that they were slumming. Not for us the small-brim hats and curling-comb-sausage hairdos. If it wasn't Byron Lee and the Dragonaires' cha-cha-cha and twist, then it was Carlos Malcolm's rock and roll. I was not allowed to socialize below Cross Roads, so I enjoyed my ignorance and danced the rock and roll enthusiastically.

Grab, step, spin, return.

Grab, step, spin, return.

Praying the elastic in the waist of the crinoline wouldn't snap under the weight of the dried starch which stiffened it and which scratched the soft skin behind our knees with every swirl. In our group, Saturday's female teenage preoccupation was ensuring that the crinoline was washed, starched and stretched out in a circle on the line in the sun from early morning, so that it would be dry and crisp for the afternoon matinee at the Carib cinema.

Also washed and dried to a crisp was our processed hair, creamed in imitation of hairstyles we saw in the movies at the Carib. We would swirl and swirl until the end of each number, then return to our seats around the dance floor to sip rum and Coke and dab the sweaty hairline, leaving the floor to more skilled and energetic dancers.

Then came Saturday night parties that, if one was lucky enough to be invited, were considered successful if the popular set of White Canadian and English men attended — that group of hedonistic new immigrants to Jamaica whom all the city's beauties were earnestly pursuing as husband material. Just as we had been trained at our upper-class schools to copy White norms of beauty, it was drilled into the psyche of all of us 'well-brought-up' young ladies that we should try as best we could to find a White husband. ('Make sure the children come out with "good" hair, my dear.')

The Canadian and English boys never had it so good. Imported by the island's upper-class businessmen who were beginning to develop the newly 'Independent' Jamaica, they were advertising executives, architects, doctors, engineers, teachers, clerks. Once their initial culture shock had worn off, they rapidly became accustomed to being in great social and sexual demand, and many rushed to take marital advantage of their singular good fortune, scouring the annual beauty contests for their prime selection.

The beauty contest was a rite in which the city's most beautiful young lady would be persuaded to compete against an assortment of popular beauties whose cheering sections featured the city's most notorious playboys. It was an extravaganza of poolside fashion parades, social appearances and dramas, culminating in a splashy 'coronation', at which the 'lady' would graciously accept victory over the popular beauties, whose tears of defeat would quickly be stopped by expensive presents from their playboy friends.

I devotedly attended each coronation, sighing wistfully at these parades of confidence and beauty that came from being 'almost White' and with a 'good' figure and, especially, 'good' hair – the requisites for all beauty contest entrants. I kept my swimsuit for the rum punch parties at friends' homes, the pools of favourite small hotels, or the popular beaches – all of which were Sunday's diversions.

Sundays would end back at someone's house, drinking beer or white wine, eating boiled lobster or packaged pizza, before getting back home to prepare for the mundanity of Monday.

Life for this particular young Jamaican had no certain plan. It was enough that I had been bold enough to start living on my own – one of the first young Jamaican women to do this. Sharing a Mona Heights back house with a former schoolmate, we quite shocked 'society' – not only by this daring act, but by the fact that we liked to walk barefoot, drive to a beach to watch the sun set, or play our guitars at bohemian parties in the fashion of folk singer Joan Baez, whom we admired, in the company of our multi-racial friends. Otherwise, life was mostly lipstick, nail-polish, clothes, boyfriends, parties and music. And occasionally, some silence to read, and think, and dream.

But though the circle was being increased by White men, it was decreasing because of immigration. Friends were leaving, following the working-class trend to seek a life outside Jamaica. As the banana boats filled with immigrants for the streets of London and Birmingham, so the airplanes filled with Jamaican girls leaving home. The lightest-skinned girls went first.

To Canada. America. England.

To study, they would say.

To work.

But really, to look for a husband.

To pretend to be all-White, not just nearly.

Then the bolder Black girls departed.

To New York.

To Germany.

To Italy.

Hoping for a life in 'show business'.

As a model, they would say.

But also looking for a husband.

Definitely not Black.

And the girls for whom Jamaica was suddenly too small.

An indiscreet pregnancy.

Sad love affair.

Possessive boyfriend.

Possessive parent.

Yes, Jamaica did seem very small. Why, one crazy Canadian could drive from Kingston to Montego Bay in three hours! Wet your knickers, if you were in the car with him. Or scream in anger at his disregard for death's possibility – yours, his and the humble people walking on the dark country roads whose lives he nearly ended. And sometimes did.

Yes, Jamaica was very small. Four hours small. And repetitive. And always the feeling of not fitting in, not being a part. Not enough challenges, opportunities. Still just a one-horse town, two years behind American fashions, movies, shoe styles, hair styles. The only thing up to date was the music. The Jamaican Top Ten was almost the same as the New York Top Ten, except when one of those ska numbers would creep in, like 'Guns of Navarone' by that revolutionary new Jamaican group, the Skatalites. But mostly it was pure rock and roll.

So, on to the next party.

Sew up a dress on the Singer hand machine.

Buy a new lipstick.

Pray that the hair would look good.

That the special crush would be there.

That I wouldn't be a wallflower.

Again.

'Come On Baby Let the Good Times Roll'.

God forbid that any serious thoughts should be uttered in all this superficial frivolity. It was bad enough that I had been branded with the slur 'intelligent', which threatened to set me apart as if I had a communicable disease, until I wised up enough to hide any signs of a functioning brain underneath the norms of rock and roll camouflage.

I wanted friends.

I wanted to fit in.

Being thin was enough of a handicap, without being intelligent too.

In the midst of all this circle of nothingness, my friend Beverley Anderson – yes, the same Beverley Anderson who later married Michael Manley – phoned to ask if I wanted to be in a film. In those days she was working as assistant to Perry Henzell – yes, the same Perry Henzell who later made *The Harder They Come*. He was making TV commercials, and hiring himself and equipment out to foreign film crews working in Jamaica.

'Don't you speak Spanish?' she asked.

With an assurance born of Miss Feres's Spanish classes at Wolmer's Girls School, plus shy practice conversations with some of the hundreds of Cuban youths whose parents hurriedly sent them to Jamaica to prevent them from running away to the Sierra Maestra mountains to help Fidel fight his revolution, plus subsequent stints as translator for some of the middle-class Cubans fleeing the triumph of the revolution en route through Jamaica for Miami, I said yes.

'Some people are looking for Spanish-speaking girls to act in a film,' she said excitedly. 'Twelve pounds a day. You want to come along?'

Twelve pounds was what I earned in a week. My desire for such money far outweighed any hope I may have hidden in my extremely flat chest to become a movie star. I put down the phone, trotted around to Personnel, and arranged to take two weeks' vacation from my job in the PR department of a leading advertising agency, to coincide with the film schedule.

The film was *A High Wind in Jamaica*, the Richard Hughes novel which tells the comic-tragedy of an inept pirate who inadvertently captures some young children en route from Jamaica to England. A love-hate relationship develops between them, which eventually leads to the death of one child and the pirate's capture, trial and hanging back in England. Directed by Alexander Mackendrick, starring Anthony Quinn and James Coburn, and later to become a classic, it was not the first film to be shot in Jamaica, but the first to be authentically set in Jamaica.

I and the ten or so other 'Spanish-speaking' girls had been cast as 'ladies of the night', and our segment was to be shot at a site on the main road between Ocho Rios and Montego Bay at a place called Rio Bueno – an old former slave port with a collection of picturesque limestone block buildings dating from the sixteenth century. There, an old seafront warehouse had been re-thatched, while on the opposite side of the road a similar old building had been converted into a rum shop and inn labelled *Damas de Noches*. The building not only served as a set, but was also storehouse for props and costumes, stars' dressing rooms and a senior personnel canteen. Both buildings still stand at Rio Bueno.

They bundled us off downstairs into 'wardrobe' where we were given our costumes. I was given a soiled, tatty pink and white striped dress with a pink ostrich feather, but my air of inno- cence was so apparent that, after one look at me, the wardrobe mistress scurried me back downstairs and gave me a long black wig to wear, which she felt added the right amount of tartiness to my look.

I, a nice, well-brought-up St Andrew girl, was quite ill at ease in my character. Not only did I NOT know how to be a 'lady of the night', but I refused to set my mind to imagining how such a person would act, lest my acting be mistaken to be based on real- life experience. This dilemma remained with me through all the scenes I was to be in, and I am sure must have caused the casting director (and Beverley) to wonder if they had made a wise choice in me.

For me, however, it was fascinating to be on a film set for the first time and to see the various people who made it all work. There were the White film technicians who had come out from

England, now dressed in shorts, boots and a deepening suntan. There were their Jamaican seconds, burly Black men carrying their air of importance conspicuously, in case anyone should mistake them for ordinary unemployed mortals. There were various lesser 'extras' standing around waiting for their scenes to be filmed, not in the same category as we who were actually called on to speak words – the reason for our exalted wages.

There were the second-string actors – nice Jamaican Charlie Hyatt, forever pinching bottoms and telling rude-ish jokes; Guyanese Dan Jackson, big and Black with a gold earring in his pierced ear (not a common sight in those days) and an English accent to remind you that he had come from Britain and was not like the other Black men; a nice Australian Trader Faulkner, friendly and eager to teach, especially those ladies who had misrepresented their Spanish-speaking abilities and were forever in need of Spanish phrases and sentences before any scene could be shot; and the handsome Benito Carruthers, slim and sexy, halfway between Black and White, but definitely with much larger fish to fry than us swooning Jamaican girls.

There were four young English children, the stars of the film, between the ages of six and twelve years, friendly but reserved and given to singing choruses of strange songs by a pop group with the even stranger name of 'The Beatles'. There was the exotic and aloof Viviane Ventura, a mini-starlet playing the eldest of the children, given to much posturing and changes of clothing and who everyone thought was very tiresome, but who was clearly convinced that this was the movie in which her Elizabeth Taylor-like beauty would be 'discovered'.

And then there were the real stars of the film – the tall, sandy-coloured and devastatingly handsome James Coburn, in the film which led to his international stardom and roles in the *In Like Flint* series. We could only dream and admire from a great distance this 'golden god', who was a bit aloof though very pleasant.

We girls reserved our real love for the Big Man himself, Anthony Quinn, playing the chief pirate and totally dominating the entire film and set. The character of the happy bumbling pirate fitted in exactly with his personality, and – surrounded on all sides by prima donnas and stars – Quinn was the most totally down-to-earth and human person above all others on the set.

His favourite pastime between scenes was to play the 'Truth Game' with all comers. In my primness, I only got a chance to sit in once with the regulars, because it was a no-holds-barred exercise in finding out as much personal information as possible about the players, without revealing too much of your own.

I was too easily shocked a person to be a good player, and too naïve to understand the nuances of some of the sexy questions and answers, so eventually I found myself outside Quinn's magic circle, only able to listen to his bubbling laughter and the giggles of the other girls from the other side of the wall of his dressing room.

But there was an advantage to this segregation of mine, for it caused my friendship with the wardrobe mistress to deepen, until I discovered she was really the wife of the film's director 'Sandy' Mackendrick who had merely been helping out on a rushed wardrobe morning. My return visit to the wardrobe mistress had opened up a slight friendship between us, since she was less rushed on my second trip. We talked about England and I told her of my desire to live there – a desire held by almost every ambitious Jamaican at that time of high immigration fever. She in turn told me of the shops I should visit and the things I should buy, if I ever got there. Woman talk, and harmless, but little did I realize how useful it would be.

We talked more about England whenever we met, until one evening as I was walking through the lobby of the hotel where we all stayed, she called me over, introduced me to her husband and asked me if I would like to go to England when work in Jamaica was finished to be an extra in the interior scenes of the *Damas de Noches* set.

Would I?

Rhetorical question.

It didn't take long for me to make the arrangements. In two weeks I had resigned my job, told my boyfriend, as well as my father, packed a suitcase and set my mind to becoming a resident of London, England.

My boyfriend was a bit sad – we had been together for four years, but things were beginning to deteriorate. My father was not at all pleased. In his opinion, my life should be lived from the safe prison of his house, until such time as he selected a suitable husband for me.

My move out of his house two years before had not only incurred his wrath, but his sulky silence ever since – equated to my mother leaving him some fifteen years ago at the end of their marriage. Now, as he drove me, my brother Paul and my boyfriend (of whom he did not approve, as he was merely a penniless medical student) to the North Coast hotel from which the film crew was departing, the only consoling fact about his angry silence was how glad I was to be getting away from it all.

England was a promised land, a new slate on which I could write any experience of my own I wished. I would be mistress of my fate, and make all my dreams come true. I was more than eager to start. Onward, to fame and fortune!

There were just three of us who had been singled out to accompany the crew from Jamaica – my friend Beverley Anderson, as well as an actress named Maude Fuller, who had a large role in the film as the children's nanny, and myself.

The flight was calm, but eight hours long, and we landed in England on a grey London afternoon to our first encounter with the subtleties of British racism. We three had no work permits, as was necessary for regular immigrants, but as our future employment was guaranteed by the film company (at least for a month or two), we had been assured in Kingston that work permits would not be necessary according to the immigration rules then in existence.

But on arrival at the airport, British racism took over. We were separated from the rest of the crew, directed to individual cubicles, and there made to strip completely and be searched. We covered our feelings of humiliation with the thought that this was standard practice for new arrivals, and when the big White woman poked her fingers up my private place, I cringed in shame yet considered the invasion in the same way as bitter medicine that heralds a cure. It was not until we compared notes with other Jamaicans in London and discovered that they had not been subjected to such humiliation, that we realized that in the eyes of the immigration officials, we were no more than prostitutes whom they were examining for venereal diseases.

Why else, we assumed they assumed, would three pretty Black girls be travelling in such fortunate circumstances with so many White men?

We emerged from the terminal all alone. A car was waiting to take us to a hotel in Kensington, and we drove in silence into London, through the grey light which was neither dusk nor dawn but the all-day colour of the English September day. Suddenly, I felt small, helpless and alone. Not for one moment did I regret my decision to come to England. It was just that suddenly I realized that I was on my own to fend for myself among these hundreds and hundreds of White faces, none of whom looked at me with the slightest bit of friendliness. It was a sobering realization to contemplate as we drove past the houses, gardens, shops and people of London.

Chapter Two

One particularly English puzzle confronted me in my hotel room. I could tell from the neighbourhood that we were staying in a fairly upper-class place. The street on which our hotel was faced Hyde Park, and there were expensive cars parked down the centre of the broad avenue. The desk clerk was suitably aloof to make us feel that she was accustomed to dealing with far more important people than three Black Jamaican women.

Which made it all the harder to find the solution to my problem, which was: as I prepared to go to bed, I washed my face and brushed my teeth in the basin in the bathroom attached to the room, but where was the toilet? There was indeed a bath and a basin, but search high and low, I could not find a toilet. I looked under the bed for a chamber pot, but found none. I looked again in the bathroom, tapped every wall, searched under corners, in case I was overlooking some simple device, but eventually I had to conclude that in designing this particular room, the hotel had neglected to put in a toilet.

With much trepidation and unease, I perched on the edge of the bath and relieved myself of the day's accumulated liquid.

The next morning Beverley and Maude were hysterical when I told them in hushed tones the story of the missing toilet. Finally they gathered themselves together enough to explain that up a few stairs on the landing was a toilet to be shared by the guests on that floor. Coming from a Jamaica of luxury hotel rooms — each with air conditioning, a view of the sea and one toilet per individual — I thought this practice not only barbaric but unhygienic. I never got used to the idea of sharing a toilet in all the years I lived in England, especially the idea of sharing a toilet with a total stranger.

I can never forget my first days in London. I had bought a bottle of Diorissimo perfume in the Montego Bay airport, and the smell will always put my head back to those days. On our first day, we went to Oxford Street to buy shoes. I later regretted my two pur-chases which had looked so attractive to my unpractised Jamaican eye, but which turned out to be made of cardboard and very uncomfortable. I soon learned that choosing leather shoes was important not only because of comfort, but because what you wore was carefully scrutinized by all who saw you to determine what you were worth and which social bracket you were in. Cardboard shoes, however pretty, meant you were right at the bottom.

We were appalled by the dull colours people wore — grey, brown, maroon, navy and beige. In 1964 neither Caribbean gaiety nor hippie madness had yet affected the British culture, and it was simply not possible to buy anything in red, yellow, bright green or any of the colours we Tropical Roses were accustomed to.

On Oxford Street, too, Maude gave us our first lesson in how to detect and deal with 'colour prejudice', as racism was then termed. We were in a Marks & Spencer shop trying to buy sweaters when, after trying to attract the salesgirl's attention in vain, Maude said loudly: 'She doesn't want to serve us because we are coloured.' (In those days we did not call ourselves 'Black'.) The salesgirl looked in our direction with a haughty expression which confirmed Maude's statement. 'Keep it then,' Maude said, flinging down the sweater, and stormed out the shop, closely followed by Beverley and me.

'That's why you mustn't buy in cheap shops,' Maude explained to us on the street. 'The poor Whites who work in them consider themselves superior to immigrants, and when they have to serve you, it makes them vex.'

The whole scene had made me afraid, terrified in fact. We bought some clothes in a dress shop and I was glad to be finished, for ever I hoped, with shopping.

You know, looking back on it, the attitude to have had would have been one of patience – if they don't like serving me, well I'll wait as long as they wish to MAKE them serve me. But, gentle reader, remember these were the days before Black Power and Black is Beautiful and Black Consciousness. We were 'immigrants' or 'coloureds' and we felt that Britain had done us a big favour just by letting us into their Paradise country, so we would abide by their rules.

After all, White people WERE superior, weren't they? We were Black and second class, so we should just keep in our place. This was the mindset of Blacks at that time.

I wish I had a mirror to see myself then. Looking at pictures today of me at that age, I was certainly pretty, but I had no idea of my own good looks. In Jamaica my skinny frame had not been fashionable; in fact it was ridiculed. In Britain, many women who saw me envied my fashion-model-like shape, although I did not know that for some months, and never believed it for years. On top of my slim shape, my big eyes, shoulder-length (straightened) hair and air of innocence must have made me one of the city's most unusual beauties.

The foregoing is not said from arrogance, but sorrow at not knowing it and gaining from it a little confidence, rather than practically none. The concept of oneself as beautiful existed in VERY FEW Black people, least of all me. I saw myself as ugly, broad-nosed, emaciated, with 'bad' hair and black skin – the exact opposite of the Marilyn Monroe ideal then popular as the norm of beauty.

I wish I had known. I wish we could turn back time and live life over again with the knowledge we now have. But no such luck. To me, I was just a skinny Black (sorry, coloured) girl, fresh from Jamaica with only fifty pounds in my pocket (that rapidly dwindling), nowhere to live and absolutely no idea how I was going to conquer this awesome city and achieve fame and fortune – my real ambitions in life.

We stayed at the hotel for about five days with no communication from the film company. Eventually word came that the film would no longer pay our accommodation, and we were on our own – at least Beverley and I were. Maude was a featured actress, already a name-star in Jamaica who intended to return, so was not in the same category.

Beverley had a sister, Roma, who was already living in London in a small flat in a district named Turnpike Lane. She said we were welcome to stay, so we packed up and took the tube to Turnpike Lane.

There we found a semi-detached house in which lived the Greek landlady and her family downstairs, while upstairs there was a living room, bedroom, kitchen, bathroom, Roma, and now us as well. London seemed so big. I had never seen such wide streets. Everyone seemed to know just where they were going and what they were doing.

Would I ever know which bus to take and which direction was north? How would I begin to make friends? Where was I to look for a job? What was I going to do? I could not turn back – that I knew. But how to go forward was indeed a challenge.

Turnpike Lane didn't help either. I knew somehow that this was just not the right place to be. I was sleeping in the living room on the couch with my suitcase on the floor beside me. Roma was great, but the thought of settling down to life there was not comfortable. Roma and Beverley could laugh at it all, but I was impatient to get out. I didn't know it, but Turnpike Lane was really the end of the world. It was about five years later before I passed through Turnpike Lane again – so remote was it from everywhere else.

I had two phone numbers of friends whom I had met in Jamaica, and called them. Turnpike Lane was much too far for them to come and visit, but if ever I was in town (see how far away it was!) I should call them again. Turnpike Lane and its discomfort was beginning to be a disadvantage. Beverley agreed. We decided to look for somewhere more central.

There was something else I did not like about Turnpike Lane. It was too 'immigrant'. Nearly everyone seemed to be from a foreign country speaking a strange language. There was a flat nearby in which lived three Jamaican boys studying law and other improving skills. They had no intention of settling in England, as I did. They simply wanted to equip themselves to earn big money when they returned to Jamaica, to make themselves able to buy the house in Beverly Hills or inherit their father's business. They cooked rice and peas and chicken on Sundays and invited us over, when they would discuss the English and England and how eager they were to be back in Jamaica.

I did not share their attitude. I thought they were provincial and narrow-minded. Here was great England waiting to be explored, with so much potential for greatness in any field what-soever, and all they wanted was rice and peas and Jamaica. Had they no ambition? Admittedly, the England in which they lived was inferior to Jamaica – sad, shuffling West Indian immigrants buying smelly fish and chips outside the Underground station at nights, living in gas-metered cold flats, riding the long, endless train journey home from any civilized entertainment in central London.

But I was looking further than that. I knew that out there was the possibility for me to become a famous author, or an actress, or . . . or . . . well, something other than just another girl in Jamaica. I had had that, thank you. Surely the world held more for me. I was going to 'make it'. I did not intend to sink into the quicksand these others seemed to be fastened in. I had no idea how I was going to do it, but I was damned if I was going to sit in Turnpike Lane feeding the gas meter and trying not to offend the Greek landlady and her son.

Beverley and I phoned Trader Faulkner, who was always willing to help and offered to spend the next day flat-hunting with us. As he met us at South Kensington station, Trader looked at us with a slight misgiving. I think he wanted to warn us of what we might encounter, and in fact he vaguely hinted that we might find a little 'colour prejudice', but then again, he was with us and we didn't look like regular 'immigrants', did we. Moreover, we were film stars, not quite like other females. We started the trek around the tree-shaded streets of Kensington and Chelsea.

This was more like it, I thought as I looked at the beautiful buildings on both sides of well-kept streets. I wouldn't mind living here. But the men and women in the many estate agents we visited thought otherwise.

'Terribly sorry . . . nothing available.'

Most of them smiled that icy smile. Some smiled hypocritically, saying: 'Well I personally don't have anything against you . . . but y'know, the landlord . . .'

Or: 'Well we have one or two flats on our books, but they all say "No Coloureds".' (These were the days before the Race Relations Act made it illegal to discriminate so openly.)

Some would say: 'Yes we have several flats,' then quote us some high-priced rentals which seemed to say: Sure we'll rent you a flat if you're Black, if you're prepared to pay through the nose.

We scaled down our ambitions and tried some less fancy establishments. But these were even nastier. Finally at the end of a long and tiring day, our spirits down and our smiles gone, I burst out at one woman in whose office we had sat for at least half an hour only to be told that she didn't rent to coloureds: 'Well if you knew that's what we were here for, why the hell did you keep us waiting?'

Nasty people.

Why didn't they want to rent me a flat?

I was as good as they were. In fact, I was better.

Where I came from, I lived like a princess, goddammit.

Beverley said, 'You know what is true? I gone back to Turnpike Lane. Now I can see why Roma is content there.'

As she left, Trader remembered that the house next to his had a flat for rent. It was only a one-room bedsitter. Did I want him to ask the landlady?

Did I? The next day he phoned. It was okay. He hadn't told her that I was coloured until she had said she would rent the flat. And when he had told her, he had begged her to take me, explaining that I was a very well-brought-up girl, not a prostitute (as all attractive coloured girls were supposed to be), and moreover I was working in the same film he was in. She relented and agreed to rent me the flat at five pounds a week.

The next day I moved out of Turnpike Lane and became one of the thousands of young people living in South Kensington bedsitters. It wasn't somewhere Daddy would have approved of – one room with a bed in it (were you supposed to entertain in your bedroom?!) with a threadbare carpet on the floor, a single gas ring for cooking (also on the floor), a gas fire into which one fed shillings in order to light it, a chest of drawers and – best of all – my own private bath and basin.

The toilet was down the hall (again).

But it was considered a good address and good neighbour-hood, and at least the windows looked out over a park with trees. I unpacked my guitar and strummed my favourite song.

I was ready to begin.

Chapter Three

My parents separated when I was four (and my sister three) and I was brought up by my father in whose house I lived until I was nineteen years old. He was a widely known journalist and publisher of a monthly news magazine – the *Time* of the Caribbean – and an influential leader of his day, with enough life credits to have earned him the Order of Jamaica in his later years. Highlight of his career – in his opinion – was being chosen to present a copy of his picture book *Beautiful Jamaica* to the Queen of England on one of her visits to Jamaica.

He was best remembered for having de-segregated the pool of the city's leading hotel – the Myrtle Bank – simply by going for a swim there one day and refusing to come out despite the unwritten rule that forbade Black Jamaicans from enjoying the water. 'Call the police, call the manager, call God,' was his only comment when they told him to come out. He says he did it because a White employee of his could swim there and he – the man's employer – couldn't.

You would have thought that a father like this would have been the source of inspiration for my Black consciousness. Hardly so. What my father tried to drum into my head – successfully – was the thought that Black people could only be accepted by Whites on the basis of how well they imitated and fitted in with White customs and mannerisms, how White they could be.

My father encouraged me to straighten my hair and shave my legs. He constantly lamented the 'broadness' of my nose, and in his eyes I was considered quite un-pretty. His preference was always for White female partners, by comparison with whom I certainly fell short. This did not exactly give me confidence in myself or my looks as a Black female. By the time I was a young woman, I saw myself as ugly, thin and Black with 'bad' hair.

Ever hoping to please my father, I did my best to try to be as White as possible.

Ah well, where did we leave our innocent heroine? Somewhere in Oxford Street wondering if she would ever know which bus to take and which direction was north. An important thing to know for us islanders, which direction is north. Where we come from, our entire orientation is based on knowing which direction we are facing. If the mountains are in front of you and the sea coast is black sand, you are facing north. If the mountains are in front of you, but the sand is white, then you are facing south. In any case, where there is doubt you simply look at the sun – since it rises in the east and sets in the west, you can always be sure of compass points.

Not so in England. The sun was merely a pale greyish-yellow light that occasionally lightened leaden skies with as much brilliance as a 50-watt bulb in a large room. And those were the days when it wasn't raining. Some days the sun actually shone, but it was strange getting used to a sun that shone, but didn't give warmth.

I tell a lie. Some autumn days the sun did give warmth – in fact I learned that there could be a distinct difference in temperature between the sunny and shady sides of the street. At home we walked on the shady side. In England, I learned to reverse the procedure.

So there I was – a bedsitter of my own, a few of my precious pounds still intact, and on the road to adventure. But we were not yet finished with the film.

One day, when we had almost forgotten about it, we each got letters telling us to report to Pinewood Studios at 6.30 a.m. Trader helped to get us organized with transportation and soon we were having our first experience of a film studio. I must admit it cured me for ever of any vague hope I may have nurtured of becoming a movie star. The enormous studio sound stage was drab and boring, and the act of putting on the pink costume and black wig again brought back sharply the fact that I was no longer in the happy beauty of Jamaica – no sunshine, no between-takes laughter – just repetitive work.

We filmed the interior of the *Damas de Noches* bar sequence. Quinn was there and Coburn, and we also saw for the first time Lila Kedrova, who was to come to fame in the film she had just finished shooting with Quinn – *Zorba the Greek*. The professional English extras made us shy with their exuberant acting, the lunch was alien to us, the vast rooms and passages of the studios were draughty and confusing. By the end of the day Beverley and I could look at each other and say: 'No boy, me don't want to be no movie star.'

And mean it.

Filming over, Beverley and I never thought we would ever see Quinn again. But one evening many months later as we were walking home to a South Kensington apartment we shared, a thick fog enveloped us and in a panic we realized we were lost. Suddenly out of the mist a large figure appeared – none other than Anthony Quinn whose home we were passing! With his booming laugh, full of memories of the film, AND the Truth Game, he walked the little distance with us on the foggy streets until we were home.

I had the addresses of two friends in London. The first was an Englishman whom I had met briefly in Kingston. The other was a Jamaican girl, Sally Densham, who lived in Ladbroke Grove. I phoned her up and she said come over, so somehow I made my way there one Saturday night and had my first experience of London's main Black ghetto.

The contrasts of the city of London were sharply revealed by the difference between Turnpike Lane, South Kensington and Ladbroke Grove. Standing on the main avenue wondering which direction to turn, I was struck by the poverty, the dirtiness of the street, the shabbiness of the buildings and, most of all, by the sight of so many Black people gathered in one place in that White man's town.

And what pitiful specimens of people they were too! Loose, threadbare suits, heads covered by narrow-brimmed hats, feet shod in broken-down shoes – all wearing an air of suffering or sadness, of total dejection. Some drunks staggered past me, laughing crazily as drunks do, and scaring me. Proper brought up girl that I was, I had nothing to compare with the underworld that I felt I had descended into. It was sad and frightening.

I found the street I wanted and looked for Sally's house. All the houses were scabby and unpainted, with garbage and rotting furniture piled in the small yards outside, dying trees, dirty-faced children, shouting women, music from windows, Black and White couples, prams on doorsteps and, over everything, the smell of decay and poverty. This was the ghetto. Sally, my friend, was not in the least bit conscious of it. In fact, on reflection, I realize that she enjoyed being there, living in such a beatnik manner.

I say she was Jamaican, and I know that you immediately imagined a Black girl. But Sally was in fact White, with waist-length blonde hair and a petite Bardot-like figure. Born into one of the aristocratic English families of Mandeville, we had been tomboys at boarding school, firm friends and partners in such petty crimes as skipping classes to play 'hot potato' with water-filled balloons. Neither of us had changed much since those school days.

Sally lived in a two-room apartment with two young Australian men who worked as window dressers with her at Selfridges – the city's big store on Oxford Street. They were homosexuals and slept together in the living room, which was very well decorated – most of it with things they gleefully told me had been 'nicked' (stolen) from the windows they dressed. They thought lightly of such theft – after all, a window dresser had once stolen a grand piano!

Sally slept in the second room, which was also the dining room and opened into the small kitchen. I spent many weekends sharing a mattress on the floor with her.

There were a lot of Australians in London, I learned, most of them living in South Kensington as I was. They were clannish, given to drinking beer and considered their trip to England an essential of life before settling down for ever, so far away from anywhere, on the other side of the world in Australia. Most were simply girls and boys for whom a European trip had as much social cachet on their return home as a university degree to most Jamaicans. In this Australian community, I later met and became friends with Germaine Greer – who became Britain's first radical feminist and author of the movement's bestselling book *The Female Eunuch* – then recently graduated from Cambridge and already making a name as an unconventional and outspoken personality.

Sally returned to Jamaica a few months after I came to London, but not before she had given me a thorough introduction to the city and especially to the world of her friends at Island Records, a small music company which had been formed by her Jamaican upper-class friend, Chris Blackwell, to market the Blue Beat recordings of Jamaican ska music which was becoming popular among the West Indians of Ladbroke Grove. In those days Island operated from a small overcrowded office in Kilburn, where everyone did all the tasks including sticking labels on 45s.

Black music was not yet competing with the Beatles and the Liverpool sound, but there was a Blue Beat record named 'My Boy Lollipop' sung by Chris's protégé Millie Small, which went to Number One, and there was a group of three pretty Black

American girls named the Supremes who had a hit song named 'Where Did Our Love Go', and both songs were very popular despite a Top Ten crowded with the new stars of British music, like Sandie Shaw, Cilla Black and Dusty Springfield.

I remember Chris Phipps, an English boy who worked for Island, who amused me continually because of his very accurate Jamaican accent. I also remember two Jamaican girls named Esther Anderson and Mary Beswick who always hung out at the double penthouse flat where Blackwell and Millie lived. Both girls had starred in the 1960 Miss Jamaica Beauty Contest, achieved notoriety but not the crown, and departed for England to make their name as movie stars. Mary had changed her name to 'Martine', according to her because of the martinis she loved to drink. She starred in a Bond film, while Esther also became an actress in some minor films until she eventually co-starred with Sidney Poitier years later in *A Warm December*, but sadly neither achieved the lasting international fame they hoped for.

My world and theirs did not cross often – they laughed at my seriousness, my earnestness, my unhip ways and clothes, so I kept my distance, in awe of these luminaries who ran in the fashionable fast lanes. To be Black and part of that inner circle, you had to qualify by being rich, famous or beautiful. I was none of these. Soon Sally went back home to marry Perry Henzell and later help him make *The Harder They Come*.

(It seems my life has always been intertwined with that film in one way or another. Sally and I renewed our friendship eight years later, when Perry and Chris Blackwell asked me to handle the film's European launch. But I'm rushing the story too much.)

Chapter Four

My other friend in London introduced me to a completely differ-ent life. He was an amusing man with aristocratic connections, who was kind, friendly and loved to have me as a dinner compan-ion. I didn't realize that the most 'in' thing at that time was to have a 'spade' (Black) girlfriend. I was not his girlfriend, but his dinner and cocktail party companions did not know, and I was equally ignorant of any ulterior motive his invitations held.

For a fact, he introduced me not only to his aristocratic friends (once he phoned to postpone a dinner engagement, as his friend Princess Margaret wanted to borrow his flat!), but also to the very best London restaurants and gave me an opportunity to learn just what all those strange-sounding items on French, Greek, German, Italian and English menus were.

I remember one time I ordered 'ris de veau' thinking it was veal, to discover when the plate arrived that it was calves' brains, and he just smiled indulgently as he made the waiter take it back and bring me something else.

The best thing about my friend was that he introduced me to

the Brook Street Bureau, the leading and best temporary secretarial agency in London, phoning them up and making an appointment in his impeccable upper-class English accent for me to come in and be registered. Brook Street Bureau was an agency which hired out well-bred young ladies to offices where temporary or permanent help was required. There were many of these in the city, but Brook Street was the leading one with the highest calibre girls, and paying the best rates. I later learned that part of their reputation was because of the fact that they registered few 'coloured' temps on their books – so exclusive were they.

However, I did not know this when I went in, and they were especially polite to me, particularly after I had demonstrated my above-average typing and shorthand skills perfected in Jamaica. So now I had a job – or several jobs. Each Monday morning I would report to the Bureau at its offices off Oxford Street to be given directions and instructions for that week's work. Some jobs were far on the outskirts of the city, soul-destroying tasks to type forms and ledgers and bills ad infinitum.

'I am the temp,' I would introduce myself shyly, and then be shown to my desk and the pile of work.

I type fast and, moreover, I like to get my work over and done with quickly. Sometimes my efficiency was praised. More often I sensed a surprise and resentment at the fact that a foreigner was performing better than an English native. Most 'temps' were dissatisfied young girls who wanted to be models or get married, and who looked on temporary secretarial work as a necessary irritant on the road to achieving these goals. For me, it was not only survival, but a periscope for surveying the city and what it offered, so I gave my best.

I discovered later that a report was made on the service given by each temp. I also discovered much later that before I was sent to an office, the person requesting secretarial services was asked whether they minded the fact that I was 'coloured'.

'We have an excellent young lady – there's only one thing: she's coloured. Do you mind?'

I was working long term in a lawyers' office when I found out, and then I understood why some Monday mornings I would wait in the Bureau's reception area for many hours while girls who came in after me were sent out on assignments before me. When I found out what was going on behind the closed doors, I did not know whether to be angry with Brook Street Bureau or not. Were they apologizing for me as one would for a cripple? Were they just trying to save me embarrassment?

Eventually I decided I didn't care. Anyone who employed me soon discovered they had an above-average person in ability and intelligence.

Why did the English make themselves so difficult to be loved? I found them a cold, unfriendly, unattractive and hypocritical people, and patience and endurance were my only survival strengths. The more I compared myself with them, the more I wondered how we in Jamaica could consider them our superiors.

As I began to discover the subtleties of English accent and class differences, I realized that the Englishmen who had come to live in Jamaica, whom we Jamaican girls worshipped and whom

Jamaican businessmen hurried to establish in prosperity, came from British beginnings as humble as the West Indian bus conductors, street sweepers and common labourers who were the object of racist contempt.

Yes, travel certainly broadens the mind.

Not that I was as bold in my thinking as the above would make you believe. In fact, I was still shy of my own shadow and blessed only with a fierce determination not to return to Jamaica until I had 'succeeded' – at what, I did not yet know. Only God protected me, alone in that city and country, from harm, decadence and discouragement. Instead, I was certain that better would come. I learned a lot about London from my Brook Street Bureau jobs, and I was glad I had the typing and shorthand skills that ensured that I could always find respectable employment.

Often my Bureau jobs were with one department or other of the British Council, the agency that handled British cultural and educational exchanges between the Mother Country and her colonial outposts. In 1964 there was still a great portion of the Empire remaining, and few people thought there would ever be any change in the colonial status quo. There would always be Black civil servants to be trained in colonial ways, students to be educated in English practices and lecturers to be despatched to every corner of the Empire carrying their messages of English intellect and culture.

One of my temporary jobs with the British Council lasted for ten months, as I worked as secretary for a room of three female junior executives whose jobs handled the tuition, housing and minor needs of various foreign students from the Commonwealth.

It was in that room, listening to their comments, that I first heard expressed the polite comments of English racism.

To hear them speak without compassion or understanding of whatever misfortune had befallen one of their students – most of whom were adult men and women ranging in years up to sixty – was to hear contempt, impatience, criticism and irritation based on racial inferiority expressed as a God-given right in analysing every situation.

As a foreigner myself, I was only too well aware of the culture shock and problems of adjustment that we all encountered, but I was too shy to even begin to explain how strange things must seem for a Pakistani, Kenyan or Barbadian who had never left his own country before, or even experienced cold for the first time.

Nor could I explain – the ladies did what many people were to do to me. They included me in their conspiracy by excluding me from the criticisms of my fellow Black people, saying things like:

'But you're not like them – you're educated.'

Or: 'You're not really Black – you're almost White!'

Or: 'You speak English so well, one could almost forget you're coloured.'

Polite racism. In 1964 I had no answer. Brought up as I had been in the neo-colonial Jamaican society to regard such comments as praise, I was guardedly happy to have passed the test to remain in their inner circle, but wary enough to keep my distance. Some incidents that caused my bosses to get into quite a tizzy as they tried to sort them out, were when Asians spat on the clean Oxford Street pavements (since their culture considered swallowing your flu phlegm a nasty thing to do), or when Black men were impertinent enough to proposition an English girl on the street and cause an international incident. At these times the ladies would confirm they viewed me as upper class by assuring me they knew I wouldn't behave like these immigrants.

No sir, not me.

To be 'coloured' was a term of scorn only slightly better than to be called an 'immigrant'. 'Immigrant' was the word used to describe the flotsam and jetsam of West Indians, Indians and Pakistanis who felt the brunt of racial prejudice while suffering to survive at the very bottom of the English social, economic and employment levels. I was definitely not an 'immigrant'. Coloured, perhaps – although I did not like the phrase.

I preferred to be referred to as 'spade', which is how my small, growing circle of English friends referred to me. It was a more hip term, friendly, if you had to use one at all. But why notice my colour at all? I didn't see my own colour and I didn't mind yours, so all I wanted was for you to ignore mine too.

Few did.

Sometimes out of the gloom of cold faces, one English face would light up, smile, ask eager questions, give much-needed help. But if you questioned this angel of assistance and love, you would soon find that in nine cases out of ten she was married to or living with a Black person.

For some reason, one didn't get too close to those people either. The Profumo Affair, starring Christine Keeler and her Jamaican boyfriend Lucky Gordon, had happened only the year before and caused such mixed liaisons to be branded with the same brush. Since some West Indian women had given us the reputation of being all prostitutes, any Black men or women who were attractive, not too shabbily dressed and without an air of down-pression were automatically assumed to be 'on the game'. I stepped angrily away from those red faces which peered into mine with the unasked question leering in their eyes, and sometimes on their lips.

ME! You should be so lucky!

But all was not grimness in life. In fact, it was often quite pleasant and sometimes exciting. I looked forward to the approaching winter with glee, eagerly anticipating my first sight of snow.

Meanwhile there was London to explore, and I enjoyed the exploration. It was exciting simply to shop for food, to discover new delights such as apples, pears and plums, to see the flower sellers outside the tube stations with their beautiful bunches, to hear people talking in languages I didn't understand. I felt like a real little explorer.

I took a bus to the Tate Gallery one Sunday and walked through the rooms and rooms of paintings which I had only seen before in books. I looked at them in their reality and began to understand what it was that made each a considered work of art, saw the size of the paintings, the intricacy of the brushwork, the clarity of colour, the boldness of style, the expertness of detail, the magnificence of conception.

There were the rooms of famous Turner skyscapes and seascapes, the gentle ballet dancers of Degas, the opulent Reynoldses and Gainsboroughs, the pure Van Goghs, the sensuous Modiglianis, the brittle Giacomettis and the peculiar Picassos. More marvellous than all the paintings themselves was the Tate itself, with its huge, high-ceilinged rooms and rooms and rooms. There was so much to stare at, including the people who were staring at the pictures, and at me too.

I never got used to being stared at. Why was everyone always looking at me? It never occurred to me that it could have been because I was pretty. I assumed that it was because I was Black. 'Prejudice' was a monster I lived with constantly, making me wary of every encounter.

For instance, I preferred to take the tube than ride on the bus. Why? Because taking the tube meant that I could often buy a ticket from a machine, or if not, from a window where the seller didn't have to touch me to hand over the ticket. Then again, on the tube I could find a seat by myself on the long benches which were divided by arm rests. That way no one would have to touch me when they sat down, not because I did not want to be touched (which, of course, I didn't) but because I was told and could observe that the White people did not want to be touched by Blacks.

The bus was different. The White conductors, and conductresses especially, had a contempt in their voices when they spoke, a resentment of my being on their bus, which they openly displayed to all Black passengers. There were some who would return change carefully, so as to not touch your Black hand at all. And often, passengers would come on the bus and see an empty seat beside you and stand, rather than sit next to you.

I tried to ignore these things, to pretend that they weren't happening, but it was hard for me. I often swallowed a lump in my throat when they occurred.

Was this not the England I had been taught about in school? I had waved my little Union Jack at the Queen when she came to Jamaica in 1952. I could sing 'Rule Britannia' and 'God Save the Queen' as well as anyone. I knew the average mean rainfall of the British Isles, the geography of the Lake District, the names of spring flowers, the history of how Churchill won the war to make me free, and I had read my Wordsworth and Shakespeare to the very last word. I was no different from the English, I thought angrily.

Why did they hate me?

I hadn't done them anything.

I wasn't taking away their jobs.

I wasn't an 'immigrant'.

Beverley, Roma and I used to discuss the subject at length. As winter approached, they had found a two-bedroomed flat near mine, and asked me to share with them. I accepted eagerly. The bedsitter had been lonely, with only my guitar to keep me company on weekends. It was good to be back with people like myself. Beverley and I were astonished, angry and afraid of the hostility we met in every single encounter – whether in a crowded street, shop or in our workplaces. Everything had to be instantly assessed to see whether it represented a racist threat in response to our presence.

Roma's attitude was different. They could all jump in a lake as far as she was concerned. She didn't intend to stay in this god-forsaken country much longer. She didn't give two hoots whether they liked her or not. She didn't like them, or the way they lived. They were barbarians, and she didn't see how they could look down on her, because she was busy looking down on them. She made us howl with laughter.

The men weren't even good-looking, she would say contemptuously, as we roared with laughter. And with that condemnation, she dismissed them completely. She was definitely not interested in fitting in.

The flat we lived in was, by London standards, very nice. To us, it was typical of the substandard living conditions the English (and we) tolerated. Owned by Greeks (again!) who lived downstairs (again!), our flat was no more than one large room divided by plyboard partitions into a living room, two bedrooms and a passage – beyond which were a kitchen and bathroom, neither of which had been clean when we rented the flat and neither of which were ever to become clean, no matter how hard we tried, although we soon gave up.

It was furnished, but with what furniture! Overstuffed, frayed sofas with springs coming out of the bottom and beds with hollows in the centre. There was only one light, hanging in the middle of this big room whose rays never lit the various partitions. This meant that a night of reading a book was completely out of the question, unless you wanted to spoil your eyes. Also, one person coming in from an evening out would wake up everybody simply by turning on the light to see her way around the flat.

Most hysterical of all was the flat's wallpaper. We decided that the landlords must have used a sample book to paper the room because, no matter how we searched the nearly 100 different patterns, none was repeated anywhere on the wall. We laughed about it endlessly, but in our serious moments we realized that any notions we might have had of making the flat our home, or turn-ing it into a place we would be proud to entertain in, would have to be forgotten. We didn't even have dining chairs.

With no television to entertain us, we had laughter instead. Beverley and Roma worked at the Economist Intelligence Unit as secretaries, and they had a few friendly workmates who often visited and took us for simple dinners. They, semi-aristocratic young men generally in training for semi-diplomatic assignments abroad, or higher futures in institutions such as the BBC or the City, not only had no prejudices, but in fact enjoyed our happy and unusual company.

At long last winter came. Yes it was fun, really. It was damn cold, too. Inconveniently cold. For instance, at the British Council they had a government rule that the heating could not be turned on until a certain date in October. So no matter how cold the day was, you just had to pretend it wasn't. In my unprepared Jamaican clothes to which I had added some sweaters, I suffered in silence and wonder.

At home the heating, which was controlled from the landlord's region, was never warm enough for us. We learned to sleep in several layers of clothing, as well as blankets. Most prized of all my possessions was a pair of big fur-lined boots. They looked like chopped-off galoshes three sizes too large, and Beverley and Roma could never contain their laughter each time I put them on. It used to make me angry to see them doubled up weakly on the floor whenever they saw my skinny little legs disappearing into the unattractive black boots.

But I had the last laugh the morning after the first snow had melted into slick ice on the neighbourhood pavements, and we walked the short distance from flat to tube station. At least, I walked. Beverley and Roma, in their pointed-toed, stiletto-heeled shoes, skidded, slipped, skated and finally fell down. After that they regarded my boots with respect and a little envy.

But the snow was what made up for it all. The one beauty of our flat was that it overlooked a park, or what was called a 'square' – an area of green grass and trees planted in the middle of a row of flats and providing a breathing space for the privileged owners of keys to the entrance gate. From two storeys up, our view of the square and its trees made up for the ugly drabness of our flat.

To wake one morning and find that overnight the green below had been magically transformed to all white was a miracle indeed. I pressed my nose to the window, whose corners were piled with soft white powder, and looked unbelievingly down into the all-white world. Across the square was a line of animal prints, as if a dog had walked home through the snow. Otherwise, all was perfect and untouched. The naked branches of the trees were covered with the soft powder, and on one tree nearest the window I could see clearly how it rested gently even on the slenderest tip. It was a Christmas card picture in black and white. I wanted it to last for ever.

So this was snow!

I was seeing my first snow!

Barbara Blake, was this really you, sitting with your chin in your hands looking out at snow in London?

I couldn't believe any girl could be so fortunate, and I hugged myself with happiness. It was as if the snow confirmed that I was in England, and there to stay. Things could only get better, and at any rate they were better than Jamaica, because there wasn't any snow in Jamaica. I didn't know what the future held for me and I had no plans, except to survive and succeed. But I was quite happy, thank you.

As Christmas approached, I spent a weekend in Maidenhead – one of those picture-postcard English villages not too far out of London – with a Jamaican couple Sonia and John, and their young son. Like my friend Sally, they too were White Jamaicans, but where Sally held on tenaciously to her Jamaican-ness, Sonia and John expressed their English-ness. With their young son, I explored the Wild Wood made famous in the English book *The Wind in the Willows*. I felt quite happy to be treading in the same footsteps, so to speak, as the famous Brit who had written the book.

I guess I, too, was expressing my English-ness, nurtured in my upbringing, education and social origin. But I am now aware that it was not only this upbringing which was bringing out this English-ness, but the prejudice I was constantly aware of which seemed to cause me to want to demonstrate as much as I could how English I was – how much I deserved to be accepted, how, in fact, I was really no different at all – except for the little matter of my skin colour.

It wasn't that I wanted to be White, but that I desperately wanted to prove I could be as English as the English. I was certain that one day they all would see, and that day all the icy stares and frowns and looks of contempt would be transformed into smiles. Until then, I maintained a low self-esteem because of it. The pressure was everywhere and I was constantly aware of it.

Christmas brought with it the magic of the big city and especially the grandeur of Oxford Street – its length illuminated with the most incredibly beautiful arrangement of sky-high lights, Santa Clauses, snowflakes, reindeer, bells, winking lights, Christmas music and Christmas spirit. Sally's Selfridges store maintained its reputation for presenting the most excitingly decorated Christmas windows. I forget what theme they used that year, and Sally had long gone back home by then, but I know that I spent an entire lunchtime simply walking past each of the twenty or thirty windows and just looking, looking, looking.

The top pop song of the season was Petula Clark's 'Downtown', with lyrics that promised you should forget all your sorrows and just be happy. At that moment in time, when England and Swinging London and its music culture was world dominant, Oxford Street was the Downtown the song promised.

An Englishman whom I had met in Jamaica had written me from Kenya telling me that if some day I was to stand on Oxford Street with all the lights twinkling bright, and I felt lonely at that moment, I only had to stretch out my hand and he would touch it. I missed Jamaica and such good friends, but with such romantic thoughts for my soul to feed on, there was no time for homesickness. I spent the holiday with my friends in Maidenhead in front of a real fire, a real Christmas tree and a real colour television set showing old films, Christmas specials and Walt Disney cartoons.

I was blissfully happy.

Hair was so very important as I grew up. Hair was the dividing line between White and Black, between pretty and ugly, between upper and lower class. How I wished for a trace of 'straight' in my natty profusion. Not so.

At boarding school two kind older students would set aside one Sunday per term to wash and comb my sister's and my hair. We would be excused from lunch because the torturous combing out usually never ended until midway through rest period after lunch. They seated us both on the open-air back verandah after the wash to dry out, before subjecting us to the pain of comb-out. The pain was awful, the humiliation worse. Those were the days before conditioners, detanglers, braid oil. A big tub of Vaseline stood next to the comb, and helped lubricate the tugs.

Ninety per cent of the girls at my very top-drawer boarding school Hampton were White, or as nearly so as made no difference. Many were rich girls from Haiti, Cuba, Venezuela, Curaçao and other exotic places, whose parents were wealthy enough to send their daughters to school in Jamaica. There were blondes, brunettes and redheads with long hair, some curled, some bobbed, but all a constant parade of envy-making hair beauty. I knew I could never have such hair and bore the mark of my inferiority with resignation.

Neither my sister nor I accepted the inferior status forced on us at this super-snob school because of our colour. We were known as rebellious, always receiving 'order marks' and 'detentions' for infringing rules. My sister, being 'blacker' than me, received the very worst treatment. Anything that went wrong at school was blamed on her first, and she was ostracized and scorned for being at the bottom of the colour ladder. I could not really understand the reasons for our treatment, racism being a totally new experience, so I adjusted as best I could to the circumstances and my loneliness by devouring every book I could lay my hands on to read.

The literature in the school libraries reflected our school's attempt to perfectly imitate the best English boarding schools: Greek and Roman mythologies, histories of Europe, and English schoolgirl adventures. Accustomed to many books at home, I read my way through the entire library. What a diet! Guaranteed to churn out one perfect English girl. There I developed culturally into a Black Englishwoman.

As my first winter in London arrived, I was totally unprepared for the chilblains. But then, you can't have heaven on earth without some tribulations. The chilblains were determined to wipe out all enjoyment of my new-found heaven.

What were chilblains?

Ah, me.

No one had bothered to warn me about chilblains.

I had them for some time before I knew what was the matter. Let me try and explain.

First of all, my feet used to start getting very, very cold, so cold that I couldn't feel them at all. But at the same time, my toes would become swollen, often so badly that it was not possible to put my feet in shoes. My home remedy was to try and keep my feet as warm as possible, so I would sit by the radiator, or put my feet in a basin of warm water, or wrap them in blankets. Soon, however, my feet and toes started to itch at special points and I would want to scratch those places as if they were mosquito bites. But scratch as I did, warm them as I did, the situation only seemed to get worse, until I was a mass of agony from the tip of my toe almost to my knees.

By the time someone explained that poor circulation, tight shoes and winter weather had caused tiny blood vessels in my feet to swell, shrink and leave behind blood clots, and that the worst thing to do in such condition was to apply heat, the damage had been done and I became a permanent sufferer of winter chilblains. The first winter was the worst. Some days I had to stay home from work, as none of my shoes would fit my feet, nursing my toes in an agony of wanting to scratch and knowing that if I did and burst the skin, the situation would be worsened. That's when the boots came in handy.

Agony! Sorrow! I made a joke of it, which made Beverley and Roma laugh.

But they didn't laugh too much at winter. Every day more and more they complained about England, about its unfriendly people, strange ways, sub-standard living conditions and climate. Finally it was too much for them. Roma was adamant and Beverley, having nearly finished a one-year course in film editing, shrugged her shoulders and off they both went back to Jamaica.

So I was on my own again. I didn't mind. The adventure was continuing and I was in its power. I found another flat two houses away, not much cleaner, same shabby furniture and sharing a bath this time (again, unfortunately). But I had been happy to find accommodation after my experience with answering advertisements in the daily papers.

'Hello. I'd like to inquire about the flat you have advertised,' I'd say in my best English. The person at the other end of the phone would explain details of size, fittings and location.

'I'll come and have a look at it. There's only one thing – I'm West Indian.'

There would be a silence at the other end while the person thought.

Then they'd say: 'I'm sorry – I'd forgotten it's already rented.'

Or: 'Well, I wouldn't mind, but it's the owner . . .' or . . . 'the neighbours' . . . or just plain simply: 'No, we don't rent to coloureds.'

After a couple of these responses, one understandably began to get discouraged. It was worse if you presented yourself in person, following an address copied off the noticeboard outside the tube station. You would think that if they actually laid eyes on you and saw that you were not a prostitute, not poorly dressed and not too Black, they might let the flat to you, but it was worse for your psyche to actually see the pleasure on their faces as they told you their lies and excuses.

Some had the grace to be embarrassed. 'Look, love,' they would say in a kindly voice, 'if it was up to me, I'd let you the flat, but you know how it is, don't you?'

I wanted to shout: 'YES I KNOW HOW IT IS! YOU'RE ALL BLOODY COLOUR PREJUDICED!'

I wanted to tell each of them how when they came to my country they lived like kings and queens in the best houses with the best maids and food and cars and privileges, just because they were White and English. I wanted to tell them that at that very moment, the most expensive hotels in my country were full of people like them being waited on hand and foot by people my colour who were eager to please them and make their stay in my country as unforgettable as possible. I wanted to ask them why, if we didn't hate them when they came to my country, did they hate me when I came to theirs. But I couldn't say any of that at that time. I could only think it.

Worse was still to come when I decided to place an advertisement in the paper myself. This time I stated 'West Indian girl seeks furnished bedsitter,' and gave my phone number.

It is true that one can only learn from experience. I received just two phone calls. One was outrightly obscene. I hung up in fear.

The second caller said he had such accommodation to offer. What was the price, I asked. He would phone back. He did.

'I am a photographer,' he said. Then he stumbled on slowly and I, uncomprehendingly, listened.

'Well if you would be prepared to pose for me occasionally, I would let you have the place for free!'

It took a second or two for his meaning to sink in.

'No thank you,' I said quietly, and hung up.

Chapter Five

I changed jobs too, going to work as a secretary for a real estate company in Sloane Street, the posh shopping street which served the wealthy Knightsbridge and Sloane Square residential areas. This real estate company was run by two debonair Englishmen-about-town who were constantly being mentioned in the society gossip columns. What was interesting was that the land they were selling was in Jamaica and their chief purchasers were Jamaicans. I have no doubt at all now that employing me was done to present a good Black image, because the operations of the company were extremely suspect.

First of all, the land where they were selling lots was a very barren, inhospitable section of Jamaica, scrub and rock hillside where little or no rain fell. On paper, the subdivision looked quite proper – neatly laid out roads, drainage, power lines. But it was some time before I realized that I was one of the few who knew what the place actually looked like. Most of the humble Jamaicans who were laying down their deposits were ex-small farmers who had sold their fertile country plots in Manchester and Portland

and St Catherine to seek a life in England that was not so hard and offered better amenities for their children. They knew no other part of Jamaica than their own country parts, and assumed that all Jamaica was as fertile as where they were from.

What was worse, the financial transactions of the company were not well kept. Occasionally an irate Jamaican who had been home to see his land would come in and demand his money back. On those occasions his loud remonstrations would be soothed by his being ushered into the inner office, by the suave English accents of the company directors, by a drink and an 'explanation' and, if all the powers of persuasion could not convince him to maintain his payments, he would very reluctantly be refunded.

More often, innocent buyers would come in complaining that despite having paid their deposit, they still had not received appropriate papers, receipts, titles and such things to assure them that they were indeed possessors of land. What would usually be the case was that the salesmen and saleswomen would persuade a man to part with deposit money, and this deposit money would immediately be taken by the salesperson as their 'commission' on the sale. This way, little money actually came into the company to pay the bank loan, so the bank was forever trying to regularize the proceedings and at the same time there were no funds with which to pay lawyers to legalize the transactions.

There were a lot of puzzled and conned would-be landowners in the Black ghettoes as a result of the workings of that company. To this day, the subdivision stands naked on the hillside in Jamaica, a large sign the only indication of the existence of so many Black people's dreams. Not a single house has been built and, isolated as it is from water and electricity, one wonders when – if ever – it will be developed.

However, it was in that office that I met Carl, a bubbling, happy-go-lucky Jamaican who was well versed in all the tricks of life as a Black Londoner. He instantly decided to adopt me as his sister and give me guidance. To begin with, he took me into some seamy clubs run by his friends, pointed out a few prostitutes and their houses to me (I am sure he had one or two working for him, although I never dared ask), and introduced me to all the inquiring males and females as 'my sister, she's a lady.'

He was a true friend, giving, giving, giving all the time. He took one look at my shabby flat and immediately used his contacts to find me a flat in posh Ebury Street, a neighbourhood within walking distance of Sloane Street and just as respectable. The fact that the flat was a humble one did not matter. Perched on the top floor of the building above a travel agency on the ground, it was newly painted with clean new furniture and carpeting on the floor. I think Carl knew of it because he had known the former (female) occupant, but I was the happy recipient of this great fortune.

This was truly a bedsitter – one large room with a bed in one corner, a two-burner gas ring and washing-up sink in another, and a table with two chairs. But best of all, just outside my door on the landing was my own bright, clean bathroom with bath and toilet together in one room that only I could use. I kissed Carl thank you right on his fat shiny lips.

It was Carl also, who introduced me to St Clair's Hairdressing establishment in Paddington, where Lorna from Jamaica and her husband George from St Vincent patiently and lovingly straightened, washed and set on rollers the hair of West Indian women – and men! – daily. Finding a good hairdresser who could do Black hair was a rarity in London in those days. Hot comb pressing abounded in the ghetto homes, but there were – at the most – three establishments where the art of cold straightening was practised, and practised well.

The little room, with its smaller cubbyhole downstairs where George did the 'creaming', was shabby and often overcrowded, but George and Lorna worked hard and gave good service. They have both persevered so well that today they have several modern establishments all over London, as well as a catalogue of hair and beauty care products, a school and a national reputation as the number one Black hairdressers. They deserve every single thing they have got. To show what good people they are, they maintain a White clientele which is almost as large and certainly as faithful as their Black clientele.

In those early days, it was amusing to see big, strapping bus conductors or masons or entertainers, and even pimps, sitting under the hairdryers among the women, with pink and blue curlers in their hair, cotton wool over their ears and a hairnet tying it all down – all in the name of style. I used to have to hold the maga-zines in front of my face, so that my giggles would not be seen.

From Carl, I got my first television set. It wasn't the greatest or the newest, but it was a television set that worked, and it meant that I had something to keep me company at nights. English TV was good, and the BBC made high-standard programmes. Some-times Carl would come over with his Jamaican friend 'Pepsi' and perhaps a girlfriend of theirs, and I would cook something or other on the very small hotplate, and we would drink a bottle or two of wine and have a nice evening.

Carl never made a pass at me and I loved him for simply being happy to be my friend. He said girls like me were rare, especially in England, and I should stay just the way I was and not let anyone or anything spoil me. I was humbly overjoyed.

Gradually I began to get to know London, ceased to be terrified of its vastness, got over my fear of getting lost on the Underground, and finally learned how key centres and neighbourhoods linked up with one another. Soon, I was able to emerge from the darkness of the hurtling underground trains, into the comparative light above ground and travel on the red double-decker buses. The buses not only had the advantage of a view of this interesting, bustling city, but best of all, on the buses I didn't have to avoid the eyes of the passengers opposite or standing upright jammed against me. On the tube I learned how to avoid looking at people and how to concentrate instead on some reading matter, or in the subconscious world of one's thoughts, for to stare was rude, however unavoidable.

London was such a variety of interesting places. At the centre was Oxford Street – a long avenue stretching as far as the eye could see, with shops carrying clothes and items of every description. Oxford Street was where all visitors from out of town or abroad shopped. It contained the famous Marks & Spencer, which sold good-quality woollens and underwear at low prices. No one, high or low, was ashamed to be seen buying 'Marks-and-Sparks' knickers.

Almost next door was the enormous Selfridges – the Harrods

of the working class. Every floor of its laden departments was a treasure trove, and since it didn't contain the snobby sales clerks and customers of stores like Harrods, one could wander around in it as one would in a museum. The famous Selfridges windows were always a shining example of the window dressers' arts, and a stroll past them was often my lunchtime treat.

Oxford Street was intersected by Regent Street, which catered to a wealthier set. One of its stores was Liberty, famous for its specially designed fabrics which were a status symbol. Liberty contained very expensive presents and household items, including silks and brocades from India and China and such exotic places.

Down the street was Jaeger, the store for suits and winter clothes suitable for the woman who is part of the rich country set. At Aquascutum and all the discreet tailors on Regent Street, rich men bought coats and ordered bespoke suits, Shetland sweaters, cashmere scarves, while at Garrard, the Queen's jewellers, I didn't even dare press my nose to the window and stare at the gaudy treasures displayed therein, lest I be mistaken for either a jewel thief or a wide-eyed Jamaican immigrant.

Regent Street led into Piccadilly Circus and Soho, the famous triangle of traffic, theatres, sideshows, peepshows and drama. Under the statue of Eros, which floated like a guardian angel in the centre of the Circus, one would always see young people gathered, squatting on the steps with their heavy backpacks resting by their hiking-booted feet, or lovers – wearing the pointed-toed black Beatles boots, while the girls displayed the English tendency for fat legs and ankles. At night Piccadilly Circus was a place to be hurried through, on the way to see a film or a play, or rushing to meet friends at a restaurant, for to slow down in Piccadilly Circus was to be accosted in many ways – all unpleasant, and one did not want to be considered 'on the game' as they said all Black women were.

But even with its sordid life, Soho had a respectable side, for it contained hundreds of good restaurants of all nationalities and prices.

The Italian and French were top of the list. The Italian restaurants were noisy, bright places full of cheerful waiters and food, while the French were dark, discreet places with reputations larger than the small rooms in which they served the world's most highly regarded cuisine. There were Hungarian restaurants, Greek restaurants, Indian restaurants and, my favourite of all, Chinese restaurants such as the Lee Ho Fook and the Dumpling Inn, which specialized in steamed baskets of meat-filled dumplings and a mouth-watering assortment of really good, cheap food.

From Soho one would turn back to the city centre by way of the exclusive neighbourhood of Mayfair, where the truly rich of London lived in large mysterious buildings on impeccable avenues with quaint cobbled streets which had originally housed stables for horse-drawn carriages, but which had now been converted into very fashionable flats. The meat and grocery shops of Mayfair were filled with luxury foods, while Mayfair also housed the jewellery and clothing stores for the really rich.

Travelling from Marble Arch down the famous Park Lane housing the Dorchester Hotel, one arrived at Knightsbridge, another shopping centre for the rich, and then Sloane Street to Chelsea and the famous King's Road.

The influence of the Beatles' music and fashion had only just started emerging in the King's Road, an ordinary suburban street being transformed into the shopping window and mecca of 'Swinging London'. The entire street was changing into boutiques selling a wide assortment of trendy clothes, shoes, accessories and knick-knacks. Designers like Barbara Hulanicki, Ossie Clark, Mary Quant and some whose names have disappeared without a trace, were turning out clothes in daringly bright colours, skirts high above the knees to match geometrically cut hairdos being made fashionable by the new wave of hairdressers like Vidal Sassoon.

King's Road was becoming a regular Saturday afternoon fashion parade, as the trendies would buy new clothes to wear to their afternoon lunch dates at any of the little new restaurants along the road. From King's Road through South Kensington to Notting Hill Gate, scene of the famous race riots of the late fifties – now a fashionable neighbourhood composed of an equal mixture of beautiful upper-class homes and scabby decaying houses in which lived poor White and Black people.

By the time one had journeyed to Ladbroke Grove at the farthest end of Notting Hill, it was time to return home to Earls Court – bedsitter land – pick up my guitar and sing to myself as I contemplated the four-walled interior of my little piece of London.

Of course there were times when I did tourist things, for this was part of a London education, and acquiring the education was easy and pleasant. Special places, like the Tower of London where I could see the real Crown Jewels which I and my classmates at boarding school had to duplicate in papier mâché to decorate the school for Elizabeth's coronation. Or there was the Royal Observatory at Greenwich – an enormous and airy park on rolling hills beside the Thames, where Britain's naval power had its headquarters and which still retained all the trappings of the days when Britain ruled the seas and controlled the Empire.

I learned not to be afraid of being by myself and going places on my own, for there was a behaviour code for single girls who did not wish to be molested which was respected by all, and it was not as unusual to see a woman alone in public as it would have been in Jamaica.

I also often had the company of Indian friends, with whom I would explore the exciting and new tastes of curry – vindaloo, dhal, dhansak, chapatis, samosas – I could never tire of Indian food, especially because it was cheap. But there were also many little restaurants near my bedsitter serving cheap, wholesome food like chops and potato chips and wet cabbage, spaghetti, cold meats and pies, which catered to the thousands of young, single, lonely and impoverished young girls and boys like myself.

Not for me the vast array of goodies I saw displayed in such profusion in London. My pocket only afforded me simple pleasures, best of which were the beautiful new flowers I was getting to know and love – scented peonies like overblown roses; multicoloured anemones with their black centres; pink and white and red and yellow tulips; roses of all colours and sizes – all for a few shillings would bring a flash of sunlight to a winter-dark apartment. And in spring there was the great pleasure of the elegant daffodils, perching their golden lace-rimmed heads on straight green stalks, and making me understand immediately the meaning and inadequacy of Wordsworth's poem in praise of their simple beauty.

There were men friends who would take me for evening drinks to picturesque pubs on the riverside, or for Sunday morning walks down Petticoat Lane in the East End, or to folk-singing sessions at bistros in Chelsea and Hampstead. Joan Baez, Pete Seeger, Peter, Paul and Mary, and Bob Dylan were all the rage and the Beatles were still a phenomenon. Some would take me to the ballet at Covent Garden.

My genuine squeals of delight at these new experiences pleased them too. But I know I broke a lot of hearts because I just did not find any of them interesting for more than a short while, and was too untutored in the ways of woman to know how to begin to understand how a man showed love and how to show it back. In any case, I wasn't ready to settle down and I certainly hadn't met my dream man yet.

Someone who wondered if I had had enough of England and was ready to settle down was my boyfriend from Jamaica. For a certainty, he had at one time hoped I considered him my dream man. A medical student, he arranged to do a three-month attachment at one of the big London hospitals and turned up in March on my doorstep. I know he had pulled some strings to get there, and in addition his being Canadian surely helped.

I was glad, and not glad to see him. He had been my man for four years and we had both loved each other in a relationship with many ups and downs, but I could not accept the prospect that our relationship should lead to me becoming the wife of a Canadian doctor in British Columbia for ever more. I wanted to 'accomplish something' before making such an irrevocable move.

Still, it was good to see him, and warm and comforting to have his gentle and solicitous love again. While studying at the hospital, he made arrangements for me to have an examination and later a free operation, for the cause of persistent pain in the region of my appendix. After some eight medical students had examined my naked body for at least half an hour, the surgeon in charge, who was a noted Harley Street specialist and author of one of the leading medical textbooks, stroked my stomach one more time and promised me a small scar if the West Indies won the Test match they were currently playing. I thank Frank Worrell for an invisible scar.

But my boyfriend hadn't really come to win me back, more to check out how I felt about an action he was about to take. He told me one night that he was in love with a girl I didn't not know, had asked her to marry him, had gained her parents' consent (which mine, we both knew, would not have given). He was going back to Jamaica to marry her, he said. The best thing about her, he said, was that she was a virgin. He had always wanted to marry a virgin.

I was hurt that he could say he loved me so much, and yet find a girl to marry so soon after I had left Jamaica. Our relationship had many worries, mainly because of my youth and inexperience of life, but I knew that he wanted a Jamaican as his woman – no Canadian woman would ever please him, he said, and it was true. What hurt most was his pride in the fact that she was a virgin. It made me feel soiled and imperfect.

The funny thing is that we stayed in touch for many years after, and in one letter he confessed that sexually his marriage was a failure. He discovered that the reason why his wife was still a virgin was that she did not like sex at all. They have had no children and are divorced today. How ironic life is!

But despite my dismay, I could only accept the situation. After all, it was I who had left him and Jamaica. It would have been unfair of me to expect him to wait around until I was ready for him, if ever. So, as if in the closing hours of a swell party, we laughed and loved and enjoyed the pleasures of London that we could afford on his student savings.

It hurt bad to see him go, hurt so much that I spent a very long afternoon peering over the side of Westminster Bridge to see if I could, or possibly should, jump off. There didn't seem much point in my life; it felt empty – nothing for me in Jamaica and even less in England. I stood there until dark fell, thinking, hardly noticing the strange looks of curious passers-by, before I finally made the decision to see what next life had in store for me.

I was going to enjoy life, be happy, and succeed at something. Through the night I stayed awake and thought and thought and thought. I thought about Jamaica and my family and the boyfriend. I thought about England and the completely unknown future that stretched ahead of me.

I could not look back. I had to be resolute in my stride forward. I was a journalist and I was a trained public relations person. I would be relentless in trying to demonstrate my abilities in those fields. I was going to forget about Jamaica and get to know England and its ways as best I could.

Chapter Six

After five years at boarding school in the country, our father put my sister and me into two separate schools in Kingston. School in Kingston was quite a contrast from the elite behaviour and rituals of Hampton school for ladies-to-be. Wolmer's was just plain school with no trimmings – no music appreciation class, no embroidery afternoons, no tuck parties, no Greek novels.

I had a great rapport with my English teacher who was English, and founded a historic and much-talked-about 4th Form magazine, much in the spirit of the schoolgirl escapades I had read in the boarding-school libraries. I started a Pets Club, which held a quite successful event on the school hostel grounds, but the teachers were not amused when I arrived with a bottle of earth and some earthworms as my pet and I had to throw them away before being allowed to enter.

Kingston also had other stimuli. Here was not only a majority of Jamaican girls, but here were also boys. With Hampton's ever-present chaperoning, boys were creatures one could only see when allowed at age sixteen to attend once-per-term 'dances' at

Munro, the boys' school eight miles away. I couldn't understand boys yet, coming as I did from the strict segregation of boarding school. I had no experience whatsoever of what to do about boys, how to speak to them, or how to get them to like me. Sexually, I didn't start maturing until well into my sixteenth year, and especially since my father was extremely strict, and hardly allowed any contact outside of school. I stayed away from boys – as they did from me. But not without some sighs.

You see, the problem was that with my kinky hair, brown skin and round nose, boys never looked in my direction. To them I was invisible and I was never the first chosen to dance with at friends' birthday parties – more like the first left standing alone at the side. To top off all my severe visual disadvantages, I was skinny. Today my slim model shape is all over the runways. But these were not the times to be skinny at all. It was LONG before Twiggy.

Voluptuousness ruled. In fact, the closer one looked like the reigning Hollywood queens, the better off one was.

Hollywood offered stereotypes such as Ava Gardner, Rita Hayworth, Jean Simmons, Anita Ekberg, Lauren Bacall, Natalie Wood, Debra Paget, Jane Russell, Marilyn Monroe, Elizabeth Taylor; the entire host of stars oozed desirability through their shiny pearl teeth, red lips, straight noses, blue eyes, white skins and, the most essential ingredient, their straight, floppy hair.

Poor, disadvantaged, opposite me. There were many Jamaican girls who came close to the White ideal in one way or other. Perhaps they had straight noses, or Coca-Cola legs, or light brown colour, but the best qualification for them would be the lack of curliness in their hair.

I did the best I could to try to imitate the hair. And this I did as soon as I attained my mid-teens. From one beauty parlour to another, enduring for years the breath-holding torture of an hour under the hot combs which always left their signature mark of burned scalp. I would emerge with sausage curls which I could pretend were real, flashing imaginary tresses over my shoulder casually, unable to swim, praying it wouldn't rain, that my head wouldn't sweat too much to show the telltale demarcation line between straight and real. Even so, the deception was not enough to attract any boys – with one or two precious exceptions in my late teens.

When the magic day came and I took my first pay cheque from my first job as a secretary to a Harbour Street hairdresser to undergo for the first time the new process known as 'cold straightening', I was in ecstasy. No more worrying about the rain, or sweat. No more can't-go-swimming. From now on, just one endless life of real, straight hair.

Never mind that the hairdresser made me undergo a short crop haircut, in order that the lye wouldn't burn my scalp as she tried to process my thick bush. It burned in places, but she applied a soothing pomade that soon covered the scab that formed.

I rushed home and showered my newly straightened hair, and waited for it to fall back into place like the White women's hair in the movies. By morning, minus a few bald patches where it had fallen out, I was sheepishly rushing back to the hairdresser telling her I had had an 'accident' and begging her to fix it back as it was.

As she washed and set it again with the neutralizing oils, rollers, hot dryer and final restful comb-out, I realized that straight hair was not an easy acquisition. I also realized that I was now firmly chained to the hairdresser. So I learned to save money by setting my own hair between the regular 'touch ups' of the roots. I learned also to endure fallouts, scalp burns, scabs, reddening and even baldness, all in the name of the elusive White beauty norm.

And why? It made a difference. It was more like a status symbol, it was the distinguishing line between being normal like other girls, with a boyfriend (no matter how tenuously you gave him that title), or being considered dowdy and on the shelf. I didn't intend to be left out. I couldn't help being skinny and Black. I wanted to be there with the popular girls too. Why not? So I did the best I could.

A Black man I met in my last year in England asked me one night as I fingered my straight hair whether, when I felt my hair so straight, it made me think that I was White. It was a shocking question, because it was the first time I had realized that when you really examine the motive behind a Black woman straightening her hair, that was it.

All this didn't occur to me consciously when I straightened my hair. Like wearing the latest style, or knowing the words of the latest hit song, straightening my hair was the done thing.

So why am I talking so much about hair? Because it's really the most important beauty asset of any woman, but especially a Black woman. All our life is a constant struggle to come to grips with liking the hair that God gave us. Some Black women are at the other extreme. They preen in the hair God gave them, but for other reasons. They have the kind of hair that Black women yearn for, hair that looks like White women's hair.

The process of the Black woman's self-hatred begins the first time the natty tangles are tugged at by an adult with a comb, bringing tears to your young eyes. It worsens the first time the White beauty symbol is observed, swinging her carefree, lusted-after tresses in the breeze.

Oh, what agony, the pain of wishfulness.

The sidelong glances at the envied schoolmates with 'good' hair.

The sorrow at viewing one's own tangled mass towering over broad nose and plump lips. The deceit of 'straightening', wigs and worse; the agonies of the hairdressing parlour. The shame of the ridiculous attempts at stiff versions of Caucasian hair styles . . . oh, Black women, how we play that game, and how we lose!

Some of us fortunately acquire the wisdom to see our own true Black beauty and love the mat on our heads – however stiff or however soft – simply for the fact that it is the identifying mark of our consciously Black beauty. But it can take a long time to get to that stage.

I haven't really digressed. Just taken a necessary detour around the labyrinths of my being. Hang on, for we may well be back there before long.

However, when we last left our heroine, she was perched on the edge of a London bridge, feeling sorry for herself, wondering if she would ever find someone to love her, wondering if it was possible to find a space in which she felt happy instead of sad and lonely, thinking about . . . but finally deciding that jumping would be accepting defeat, and girding her resolve to continue and conquer.

Conquer what?

Who knew?

What was known was that there was a system to be understood and then fitted into in such a way as to achieve certain goals. Where these ambitions led was very vague. I knew that I was not brave enough to face being turned down to try being a fashion model, for I wasn't confident enough of my beauty. What prevented me most of all from trying was the reputation that Black women, perhaps deservedly, had in London of being prostitutes, especially pretty Black women who gave their profession as 'model' or 'actress'. From what I could see of it from a distance, it was an exciting life, especially for those at the top.

But I just did not know the rules of that game. To me, getting a man to give you money in exchange for giving him your body, was prostitution, however glamorously hidden the game. If the men were giving money without getting bodies in return, then I didn't know how to do that trick. So I was out of that.

Most of all, I really just wanted to accomplish on my merit. I wanted to prove myself as an individual. I didn't think I was the greatest, but I felt sure there was some place of my own which I could inhabit in such a way as to command some attention and respect.

Perhaps I would write a great book and become a famous novelist, or someone would just 'discover' me on the street (one smelly, leery man once did, to my horror, shoving a card into my hand with 'dirty photos' written all over his face, but I said, 'No thanks,' in shock), and I would be transported languidly into some great starring movie role.

Sure, we all dream. But in daylight, I really hoped just to accomplish SOMETHING, not get lost in the grey eddies of this formidable city. I just couldn't go back home and tell them I had given up.

Tried it and didn't like it, I could say; but the reality would be: tried it and it didn't like me. I wanted to enjoy the pleasures of England. And there were many.

The joy of discovering any new place depends on who you discover it with. I had an assortment of friends of all kinds, mostly English. There were young people who followed the folk music movement, going to concerts by Bob Dylan and Pete Seeger and Peter, Paul and Mary. I joined them with my guitar, and learned new songs when we visited the pubs and clubs where this music was popular.

I had friends who had been at Cambridge and Oxford, who took me on trips to these most interesting relics of English history and learning, making the modern-day activities that took place there seem even more important than just pure education.

In such places you could really feel as if you were in one of those Henry VIII films, and understand what it must have been like to live in those days, or understand immediately Shakespeare's time. The aristocratic feeling the students of these institutions gained was like a heritage, and I could understand the source of the Englishman's pride in his higher education.

Some of my friends had well-off parents who lived in country homes where, with casual manner, the families would pretend not to notice how much money was spent on elaborate, elegant birthday and coming-of-age parties with aristocratic teenagers in gowns and tuxes, or with older, titled, costumed guests and tables of champagne and smoked salmon.

There were many nice, interesting things to do. I remember wandering around the vast acres of Kew Gardens with my flatmate Caroline and her soon-to-be-husband (now the Earl and Countess of Sandwich), revelling in the imitation Jamaica created in the vast space of the glass-and-steel Victorian Palm House there – a greenhouse containing all the plants I had left behind at home – peering into the glass cases of butterflies and smelling manure on beds of beautiful roses.

I remember dreamy times spent sitting by myself on summer window sills, dipping strawberries into sugar and thick cream, taking pleasure in the warm hum of the street below; or sipping white wine at a riverside pub full of self-conscious, happy people on a balmy summer evening; or wandering around the Tate Gallery, or visiting Indian restaurants and eating with fingers and chapatis. Feeling almost completely 'English'.

There was lots that was nice. But somehow the feeling of strangeness never faded. Soon after I arrived, Sally took me to a Steam Fair, a fairground where all the attractions consisted of Ferris wheels, merry-go-rounds and church organs run by steam engines. They played the most wonderful fairground music on these calliopes, and the place was a marvel to see and experience, but my own concern was to see if I could find one single other

Black person in all the acres of showground. There was not one. Look as I did, nowhere was there an oasis of Black skin and understanding eyes on which mine could rest. Never had I ever had such a feeling of total aloneness, despite the vast crowd!

That feeling repeated itself to one degree or other in my life in England. Never quite at home, therefore never quite at ease, therefore never quite relaxed. The English were always watching you, smiling with their faces but not their eyes, studying intently to see if they could see into your depths.

All of this didn't register at once, only the feeling of uneasiness one couldn't quite touch, even beneath the most apparent sincerity. Roma had said with distinct distaste that the people were cold and simply didn't like Black people. But how could they? Up to recent history, the English had been taught that the Black man was an inferior creature, only recently removed from cannibalism and living in trees, rescued (although not without some minor suffering) by slavery, to be redeemed and made into 'civilized, Christianized' human beings.

The sector of the English who best demonstrated how deeply this image had sunk in were the poor White class. Since a Black person could not be expected to have better housing than Whites, Blacks were forced to live in sub-standard housing among the poor White class who – forced to live alongside and compete with a creature they considered inferior – spared no effort to demonstrate how annoyed they were at having to rub shoulders with such 'scum', their frequent name for us.

Consider the effect of this sudden dose of high-voltage hate on a group of peasant-class Jamaicans, small farmers looking for a less arduous life, some middle-aged, not-too-well-educated wives, and their assorted (and often unattractive) children. Dedicated to working hard, forlornly comparing the scabby slum walls and barbaric plumbing of their crowded shelter to their left-behind Paradise, unable to comprehend anything except the fact that the White slave-master man, many times multiplied in this country, still had the right of rule.

Don't disobey or buck the system, nigger, or I'll whip you and put you in chains again.

Oh, some protested – yes they did – against this brutal reasoning.

They fought back, literally.

They went to jail.

Some took the easy way out and became pimps and prostitutes.

Most just bowed their heads and endured this new version of slavery, trudging to work in the mornings and bundling up to come home again at night.

Yes, there were some Whites who were not like the others, some with genuine human feelings of decency; but oh, these were so few and far between that they seemed semi-angelic when encountered. On the whole, we accepted our lot and tried to become what the English wanted us to be, Black English. This meant trying as best as possible to 'fit in', to be like Them.

Did we have an identity of our own?

Not really. Not then.

We were what our minds had made us think we ought to be, to please Them.

The better one could succeed at being English, the better one would succeed.

Finding out 'how' was the key.

It was the time of Swinging London, and I was glad and fortunate to participate in it. For the first time ever, a city became famous simply because of its lifestyle, its music, its fashions and its celebrities. One could bump into pop stars Sandie Shaw or Dusty Springfield buying a dress on Saturday afternoon in Biba – the shop for fashionable teenagers willing to try the new miniskirt style – or try on a new hat at Mr Fish boutique where glamorous, blond Michael Fish made shirts for everyone, or stroll down Carnaby Street where the Union Jack had been turned into Pop Art fashion boutiques.

London became carefree, as girls raised their hemlines, men wore brightly coloured shirts, and everyone let loose of the English stuffiness. There were a lot of changes, especially in attitudes, as young people's values took over and became the dominant emotion of the country. The Beatles were playing a never-ending procession of hit songs, all of which spoke directly to these emotions, and the country began to be a nice place to be.

It was nice to be young then, feeling light-headed on wine at some party, excited at the clothes on a Saturday morning boutique safari, happily laughing with friends. It was just nice. Life didn't seem to have a precise goal, but to be happy was the best pleasure of all. I did a lot of laughing.

Secure in my Ebury Street flat, life was sweet. There was a small would-be gourmet restaurant down the street called The

Jabberwocky after a character in *Alice in Wonderland*, which based itself on French cuisine and attracted a slightly-above-middle-class clientele, as well as the occasional eccentric. It was a small place owned by a pleasant White man and I felt no shame at accepting an invitation from Pauline, the girl living in the flat below mine, to work as she did as a waitress one night a week.

Knowing that I would make 10 per cent of the night's takings as my income just by taking and serving food orders for never more than four tables at a time, was sufficient incentive. I earned welcome extra cash in tips as well, and in time the job taught me how to cook a great chicken Kiev and steak in red wine with cream and mushrooms just from looking on and eating the chef's great handiwork. The chef was from St Lucia, while his wife, who washed up the dishes, was from Mauritius. We served red wine, white wine and, when customers ordered rosé wine, we just mixed some red into the white and brought it upstairs. No one ever caught on. Instead, their feigned sophistication often led them to comment on the 'excellent bouquet' of our hand-made rosé.

Life became a procession of flats and jobs. Ebury Street did not last long, for reasons which escape me. Lord, can I remember the others before Chepstow Road?

I'll never forget one in Ladbroke Grove, can't even remember the name of the street, where I lived for several months in a state of total revulsion, with a houseful of young Indians, relatives of an Indian girlfriend I had met at work. I shared my room with a White girl whose perpetual sobs made me sure she was recovering from childbirth and adoption – a coloured child, certainly.

That house had the filthiest bathroom I ever had to use in my life. Whenever I had to take a bath, I would first have to spread newspapers on the floor to make a clean pathway, then scrub it out with a long brush while holding down my revulsion, and then stand up in it (once with my sandals on, I couldn't bear it) and throw water over me. How they used it, I don't know. I didn't live there long. Long enough, however, to realize that as much as my girlfriend liked me (she taught me how to cook real Indian food, chapatis and all), her relatives considered me practically an untouchable and scorned my Blackness – even though my skin colour was a few shades lighter than theirs!

Crazy, eh?

I had little time to consider such reverse racism, however, but it all added to my feeling of strangeness.

Best of all flats was blessed Chepstow Road, a small – no, tiny – two-bedroom haven on the first floor of a house where I lived for more than five years. The road connected the true Black ghetto of Ladbroke Grove with trendier Notting Hill and was a melting pot area of hipper West Indians and Whites, hippies, artists, young, rich, all mixed together. It was a way-out, no-man's-land community with a character all its own, long before it became gentrified and expensive.

I would walk to the nearby Portobello Market, which was a good place to buy good food including Jamaican items such as plantains, yam and patties, as well as clothes and antiques for tourists. There were some shabby streets as well as streets with lovely houses and gardens, pretty parks, friendly pubs, all within reach of the main London centres of Hyde Park, Piccadilly, Oxford Street, etc. It was a 'good' place to live, and I was fortunate to have found an empty room in a White girlfriend's flat, thanks to another White girlfriend.

Having a Black girl share a flat with her certainly fitted in with the lifestyle of Caroline, daughter of an Anglican priest and newly graduated from Cambridge, where she had studied Persian and Arabic. She was blonde and slightly 'daffy', worked in a library, played classical music and eventually married the Earl of Sandwich, thus becoming a Lady – a fact which never fails to rouse a smile in me when I remember the usual state of her stockings.

We got along well together, such different people. She loved to give inexpensive spaghetti-bolognese-and-wine dinner parties for her fellow graduates, who would sit on the floor in our tiny space and enjoy each other's company, which is how I came to meet a lot of nice young English people, determined to change the world – especially its racial perspectives. I also met several intelligent members of the English upper classes.

Through Caroline I became friends with members of the young television comedy crew who, with David Frost as its leader, were looming on the British scene and were soon to change British TV as radically as the music of that era changed England. In those days Frost hosted a wickedly funny satirical TV show, giving us jokes rather than the serious interviews he is now known for.

He depended largely for his humorous skits on the work of a group of Oxford and Cambridge graduates who are now internationally known personalities. These were young men like Eric Idle, John Cleese, Graham Chapman – members of the crew who later became famous by creating *Monty Python*, which made them international comic celebrities, and Bill Oddie and Tim Brooke-Taylor, who became 'The Goodies', all of whom were then turning their backs on their excellent degrees in medicine and the arts to begin careers in TV comedy.

This group of new Oxbridge graduates also included theatre director Richard Eyre – whom I didn't then know was a descendant of infamous Jamaican Governor Eyre. He was just starting his brilliant career – paying his dues working in as many small theatres and productions as he could, his eye clearly on the prize he later received of the National Theatre directorship and a knighthood. There was also Daniel Topolski, son of the famous artist Feliks, who had made a big name for himself at Oxford in rowing and coached the university's teams for many years thereafter.

I am glad to see their success since then, and smile at the memory of them all pennilessly contemplating their future as we shared spaghetti bolognese and red wine on the carpet of our Chepstow Road flat. We have all remained friends through the years, as they grew in fame and wealth.

Caroline's set of television and comedy personalities overlapped with the stars of music and fashion I was getting to know through my own circle of friends – not frontliners necessarily, but part of the machinery. My friends and I went to listen to jazz at Ronnie Scott's club in Frith Street, and to concerts by artists like Jimi Hendrix, Al Green, Richie Havens and James Brown. These were our ways of having fun. In those days it was enough to like white wine, Beatles music and the philosophy of Flower Power, to be able to participate in a world in which those involved were giving of the best of their knowledge, their vitality and their emotions.

With Notting Hill Gate a centre of the new culture, Chepstow Road was the perfect diving board for me into what became the famous 'Hippie, Love Generation' which flowered on both sides of the Atlantic in the sixties, and I gladly embraced its beautiful, warm and love-filled philosophy.

Why not? It fitted in perfectly with my view of life as the essence of love, instead of racial hatred.

Music, colours, smokes.

Little did I know that I had originally invented the philosophy.

Black me, and all Black people.

Chepstow Road was heaven. Situated on the first floor, the flat overlooked the street with a lip balcony on which one could sit on summer days. The flat was really small. The second bedroom could only hold a single bed with enough space for a person to stand beside the bed – that was all. The living room and kitchen were equally small while the main bedroom could hold a twin bed as tightly as the small one held a single. You could hear the footsteps of people walking in the flat above. Every time the people upstairs moved out, I lived in terror of who would replace them and how heavy they would be. Once, for a year or more, life was made miserable by a clumpy Scandinavian couple upstairs; I was constantly having to knock on the ceiling with a broom to quiet them.

But it was a lovable flat, and I made it pretty after Caroline moved out to marry her Earl. I moved into the larger bedroom and hosted a succession of flatmates who occupied the little room, some of them men. This was quite allowable in a city like London, especially as I made no bones about the fact that living in my flat did not give them access to my bedroom. Friends acknowledged that these men were simply flatmates, paying half the rent, who were often better to live with than temperamental females who would make passes at my boyfriends.

(I took such a situation so much for granted that once, when a male flatmate with nothing better to do for the summer holidays came to Jamaica with me as his vacation, it took me by surprise to hear that everyone translated this to mean that I had brought my fiancé home with me. Jamaica did not know about platonic relationships.)

I had a number of good men friends like these who would take me to dinner, or who I would cook for. We would go to parties with friends and talk about life, like all young people do.

I went out with a lot of guys. Perhaps because of being brought up by a father only, I am the kind of woman who needs always to have a man in my life especially for companionship, so apart from times when I purposely wanted to be by myself, I usually had a boyfriend. Sex was often not the most important aspect, in fact many of my boyfriends had to be content to wait and wait and wait until they gave up trying to bed me, and became instead really good male friends.

Truly.

In England it was possible to have male friends who were just friends. I did. One would take me to the Ad Lib Club, the first trendy disco in London's Swinging Sixties, where I would sit in awe as beautiful women glided past laughing with one of the

Beatles, or a movie star, or a rich playboy. Just reconsidering such a scene makes me really shake my head with a smile. I was a gutsy little baby, on my first steps into the world out from behind the wall of parental shelter.

I had dived off into the deep end of the black pool of the Outside World. Inside I was terrified.

I can remember that first night at the Ad Lib, when a man had glided up to me in the darkness and whispered: 'You are the most beautiful woman here.' I had been shocked, thinking he was trying to pick me up in front of my date. But perhaps he was simply seeing a beauty that I was unaware of, coupled with the calm exterior under which my fear-filled person was hiding; behaving like a swan gliding serenely on the surface, but paddling like mad under water.

It was easy to refuse sex to these dates, upper-class types who were persistent in their requests, aware that being seen in the company of a Black girl made their friends think they were great lovers, men who expected me to be the first to make a passionate pass at them (remember the reputation of Black women), and who did not know what to do when I did not. At the height of those English circles, homosexuality was the norm and most men had not a clue what to do with a woman, other than the courtesies of dinner dates.

More to my taste were the freer spirits with tender faces who took wine under trees, played Beatles records and arrived on the doorstep with baskets of ripe strawberries. These were an education in so many subjects and they were fun to be with. Parties with winter cold outside frosting the windows, music of the Supremes, the Rolling Stones, Marvin Gaye; glasses of half-drunk red wine covering every flat surface, cigarette smoke, the floor sagging under the weight of dancers, a dishevelled girl crying in the passage . . . Meeting someone new who might, just might be . . . ah well, . . . perhaps next time . . .

I had my boyfriends, of course, enjoying the beginnings, floating through the in-betweens and feeling perplexed at the ends, never quite finding one who could be 'the one', like all the other girls around me were doing.

Yes, the men were all English, and therefore all White. I had not yet found a Jamaican man in England who interested me. The few from my social group who were living in London in the sixties were either students getting their degrees and getting the hell out of the damn place (who mostly preferred White girls, anyway), or political-leaders-in-training who did nothing but talk about how they were going to run the country when they returned and who mostly preferred White girls, anyway. I knew nothing about Jamaican politics, and was not interested then.

At the other extreme were the bus conductors, factory workers or the pimps. I was then too tender a shoot to even begin to fathom these types, whom I had never before encountered in life. These were the only available Black men then, unless one accepted the much-offered invitations of the African students who would quite seriously accost a girl and state: 'I want you to be my woman,' in a pronounced African accent, which was enough to frighten a person into running screaming in the opposite direction away from round, tribal-scarred faces, ill-fitting English suits and obviously painful shoes encasing huge feet. In 1966 no one was explaining that there might be a similarity between Africans and Jamaicans.

Garvey, who was he?

Get me away from these Africans, they're crazy!

Yes. My conditioning had prepared me to unquestioningly accept the naturalness of giving myself to a man like the man in the movies, the White man. Just like straightening my hair, picking a White partner was definitely the accustomed pathway I was expected to follow. This was what a girl of my upbringing, education and 'breeding' was supposed to do.

Crazy, eh?

No, not crazy; strange.

Strange to understand that the crowning aspiration drilled into the heads of the best of our race was, and still is, to look to White values and ideals. Generations and generations of beautiful Black women denying their best to the best of their race.

No, I don't feel guilty about my history. I had no control over the conditioning I had received all my life, and as yet I had no information of an alternative viewpoint. As I said, I simply accepted as natural the fact that my sleeping partners, my emotional companions were all White.

They were all just as nice as they could be.

Chapter Seven

One day in 1979, I was waiting for a bus on the road in the rural district of Red Hills above Kingston, when I overheard two Jamaican country boys, aged about seven years old, barefoot and dressed in ragged clothes, watch a White man drive past in a car. They thought in silence for a moment, then spoke.

First boy: 'What a way that man White!'

There was silence for a good minute.

'God is White like him!'

Second boy: 'No. God whiter than him.'

There was another long pause for thought.

First boy: 'I saw a picture of the Devil in a book. Him BLACK, you see! BLACKER THAN ME!'

Well, I've taken the typewriter out here under the banana trees in the jungle of wild coco and coconut at the back of the house. The thwack of tennis balls from the posh Trident Hotel's court next door hasn't started yet, and in the early morning all is peaceful.

Occasionally a lizard peers at me from a hanging bunch of bananas, but under the shady roof of leaves I am content and ready to continue telling you all about it like it was.

Here comes a yellow and black butterfly to say good morning.

Crazy woman, aren't I.

Well you gotta be a little crazy to have been bold enough to think that you could take England by storm, and then go out and actually do it without any money or connections, only an arrogant blind faith in your little self.

You can make it if you try.

Yes, yes.

But if ever there was a reason for my writing this book, it is in the hope that African people today – wherever they live on the planet – will learn our history so well that instead of using up energy on revenge for White atrocities towards our race, we use our strength and power instead to re-create our original African greatness.

In England, watching films was my favourite form of entertainment. Whether I was lining up outside the plush Piccadilly and Shaftesbury Avenue palaces for leading first-run films, or else at 'art cinemas' where I could see films from France, Italy or India, I was happiest sitting comfortably in the dark enjoying the special pleasures of films from all over the world in the cinemas which abounded all over the city.

There were classics like the New Wave French films of Truffaut and Godard, which everyone used as yardsticks by which to measure any new film – films like *Breathless*, *The 400 Blows*, *Jules and Jim*. French cinema was the most lively, producing film after film which left the critics and fans without superlatives to describe their brilliance.

The Italians were not far behind. Fellini had created his *Dolce Vita* exposé of the hedonism of contemporary Roman society. Antonioni had presented his visual and intellectual masterpieces such as *The Red Desert* with Monica Vitti. In Sweden Ingmar Bergman was making his broody, moody films which everyone went to see – to see if they could understand them. I never did, but at least I had to go to see what everyone was talking about.

The film I loved best was one which epitomized the mood of that time, *The Umbrellas of Cherbourg* by Frenchman Jacques Demy, starring Catherine Deneuve at the height of her fresh, youthful beauty. It was the story of two young lovers who part tragically and are then reunited, only to part again, and it was sad but happy. The film was totally dedicated to beauty: care had been taken to choose fairy-tale settings; sets and exteriors were painted in beautiful colours; the clothes and accessories of the actors were chosen for their colour harmonies. Every corner of the screen was perfect.

It was a blockbuster hit even outside France and what made the film most interesting, but strange, was that it was entirely set to music – a modern-day opera in which every word was sung. Audiences did not mind, we all lined up to see it. After my initial surprise, and then the adjustment to hearing the French words and having to look beneath the frame for the subtitled translation, I found that this seemed such a natural way of telling this fairy story made for romantics such as I. I saw it three times, crying in all the same places.

Another film which impressed was *Knife in the Water*, the first film by Roman Polanski of Poland. It was a brilliant, brooding masterpiece about a couple who pick up a young male hitchhiker on their way to a weekend on their boat and find they made a dangerous decision.

There are only three people in the film and the interaction between them is strained, tense, yet sensual. Polanski's film-making genius was demonstrated by camera work so intimate that only towards the end of the film does one wonder where the camera-man and crew have been through it all.

There were films like the Beatles' crazy *Hard Day's Night* which was more an experience in Beatle-mania than a real film. There was *Shakespeare Wallah*, a film about an English theatrical family living in post-Empire India, made by the American/Indian film-making team of James Ivory and Ismail Merchant, who later became my great friends in London and famous as Merchant Ivory Productions. There were numerous British films containing their own brand of humour, and there were films like *Alfie* starring Cockney actor Michael Caine, which were introducing to the world the new British working-class style and manners which now dominated the Swinging London scene.

I loved to scrunch down in the seat of a cinema, chocolate almonds in hand, and travel along the various fantasy routes which films offered me. And it was not a useless pastime. Films constituted an important part of the conversations of the people I knew: making comparisons between the styles of various film-makers, discussions on the merits of one foreign film as opposed to another, and decisions as to whether certain films deserved high praise or critical condemnation, were not just important topics of conversation, but a learning experience for me.

Thus I underwent another degree course of study in the University of Life.

I continued to support myself by my Brook Street Bureau jobs, where I would be as polite and as nice as possible, and where people would always comment on how fast and accurately I took shorthand, typed and worked. I tried to explain that I was a journalist, but they would only smile with a look that showed they thought I was pretending to be more than I was.

I couldn't be content to be a secretary always, though. It was honest and respectable work and I eventually got some pretty good assignments, but never staying long enough to make friends, the coldness of the English felt even deeper.

Once, through some society friends, I got a job as a secretary to a man with a scheme to encourage people to send champagne to people in hospital. Boring work, endless addressing of envelopes and typing of lists.

But there was a positive. Downstairs was the office of a PR firm, a society agency specializing in getting clients' names into posh gossip columns in top magazines and newspapers. Being so close to their office, I got to know a nice lady named Felicity Bosanquet who told me there was a vacancy for a secretary – none too soon for me to escape the failing champagne business.

Felicity used to invite me and other friends down for weekends at the country house where she and her husband Reggie – a television news presenter – lived. The house was totally 'country squire', old and big. Felicity would turn from a Knightsbridge fashion plate into a rustic lady of the house as soon as she arrived, cooking pies and game fowl and Yorkshire pudding in typical English lady form. Reggie would tell jolly stories which would keep us laughing. Their guests were the kind of people with whom I could talk about authors like Scott Fitzgerald, whose entire works I had recently read and loved, or listen to them explain the working of British politics or how to play backgammon. Those weekends were lovely moments and I enjoyed seeing how life was lived in old English houses.

It was the England of the post-Christine Keeler era, and once or twice at aristocratic parties I went to I had a glimpse of the kind of high life as it had been lived at its shocking height. I never found myself trapped in these awkward or embarrassing situations, however.

In the same way one is self-conscious in a breeze when not wearing neat underclothes, I was always aware of how out of place I was in these environments, compared with the self-assured, richly dressed female guests who laughed gaily at it all, so I never found myself even near any of the misbehaviour.

I was more comfortable at the 'trendy' parties. One always tried to be at a trendy party each weekend. The trendiness of a party was determined by either the person throwing the party, or the people who were there. For example, the most obscure person might throw a party at a restaurant with an equally obscure name, only for you to find out after you didn't go that the obscure person was actually a friend of Frank Sinatra, and the obscure restaurant was now solidly booked for weeks because

Princess Margaret, Mick Jagger, Mary Quant and Twiggy were all at the opening bash.

Or again, the party you didn't go to because the address was in a scruffy neighbourhood, turned out to have been the house-warming of Lady Something Important newly wed for the second time to some trendy Chelsea artist, and the totally astonishing house, decorated by Hockney, Heal's and that new Italian place with the chrome furniture, is the new base for all her trendy friends of whom you are not one, else you would have been there.

It was a constant race to keep up, a pleasant game played by the carefree young, and I was fortunate to be swept along quite often, trailing in the stardust of the Beautiful People.

I had taken the PR secretarial job with Felicity in the hope that I would eventually move up to some larger responsibility and opportunity to use my journalism skills. At that time, it did not occur to me that my colour prevented the boss from taking a chance on me, let alone believing that I had the training and intelligence for it. But to my mind, the office was in Fleet Street, the home of British journalism, and I was, after all, the best damn journalist from Jamaica.

I surely was able to make an impression in the field, I thought, as I gazed across at the *Daily Express* building. But all doors I knocked at were so firmly closed that I gave up trying.

This was the time of Ian Smith's Declaration of Independence for Rhodesia, and I remember well the day it happened. The bus I took home passed from Fleet Street towards Trafalgar Square, where South Africa House occupied one entire block overlooking this most central and important of English landmarks. In the block just before it stood Rhodesia House. Outside it was a demonstration of English people in favour of Smith's actions.

I was terrified to see, as I sat on the top deck of the bus looking down, that all the White people on the bus turned on me and snarled . . . yes, that's what they did . . . they snarled at me, as if I was personally one of those damn Black people who wanted to overthrow the White rule in Rhodesia. At that moment, I have never wished more that I was not Black. At least invisible, please God.

I represented at that moment everything that the English 'kith and kin' (as the slogan went) of the White Rhodesians, hated. Nothing that was done after that by Ian Smith's supporters or his success at taking over the country surprised me. His success has been due entirely to the total sympathy the British had, and think they still have, with the right of the White man to control and suppress the rights of the Black people of a country they entered as immigrants.

They held a Commonwealth Conference in Jamaica in 1975, after I had returned home, and I had the opportunity of asking Harold Wilson at his press conference whether – as the Prime Minister under whose regime Ian Smith's illegal government had taken power and retained it – he supported the desires of the Black majority who were then fighting to be free. My question angered him, and he puffed on his pipe a long moment before saying that he had ALWAYS supported the cause of the Black majority, but not explaining how he had displayed this support to the British people at that time.

The memory of the Wilson gunboats to Guyana and Anguilla contrasted with unenforced sanctions on the 'kith and kin' of Rhodesia, and made him appear – at best – a Prime Minister with no power. Britain's haste to officially sanction Smith's farce elections underlined that the British attitude had not changed.

I got tired of waiting to get a PR job. I had a bright idea. Why not write a letter to the people who handled Jamaica's PR in Britain – who were they? – and ask for a job?

I found out who they were and wrote telling them about myself and my PR experience in Jamaica. Within a month I was working as a secretary to the Account Executive for the Jamaica Tourist Board account at Michael Rice & Co., a very elegant and high-class public relations company housed in what was once the home of a wealthy Park Lane family . . . Mayfair, the very best address.

Michael Rice himself was a very immaculate gentleman, with clients who were also his friends among the wealthy sheikhs of Arab nations, and governments such as Jamaica and Malta passed through the office all the time and very upper-class accents floated around the high-ceilinged rooms of those executive offices.

I was secretary to a nice gentleman with a Scottish accent. However, once again I got bored with the drudgery of the secretary's life. How did one become an account executive around here? I asked one lady. She said the way she had done it was to join the Institute of Public Relations classes for one year and take the exams at the end of that time.

A year was too long for me to wait.

When are the exams?

June.

It was April.

I borrowed her notes and books and read them. It didn't seem hard, in fact it was just as if someone had set out on paper PR rules which I already knew from practice. The exams were in four parts. I sat them in June and passed all four, entitling me to the letters AIPR (Associate of the Institute of Public Relations) behind my name. Now, how about a promotion, boss?

Mr Rice smiled. The PR Executive's assistant, Sue McManus, had gone on her first familiarization trip to Jamaica and decided to stay there. (She is still in Jamaica working in tourism.) So Mr Rice appointed me to her position and raised my salary a little. Soon, the man I worked under decided to leave and set himself up in the PR business, and I found myself with my own office, a secretary and the title of Account Executive, Jamaica Tourist Board account.

I was twenty-five years old.

Not bad.

I didn't let it go to my head, though, and become a conservative executive type. I still did crazy things, like wearing to work a short miniskirt from Biba one day and on the next the bright red sari that my Indian girlfriend had given me and shown me how to wrap. With my straightened hair, some people assumed that I was Indian. It could be fun sometimes, to be something other than Jamaican all the time.

Chapter Eight

I settled down into a quite nice life now. It wasn't grand and high style, but had enough contact with both the grand and the comfortable to make it cosy.

For instance, I became one of the Restaurant People. There were always certain restaurants which were fashionable in different ways and one stated one's mood and circle by the restaurants one frequented. I had some young girlfriends and men friends who were 'doing things' to one extent or other, who were able to afford – much as I could – to spend a little money in the proper places.

There was my girlfriend Carol Martin-Sperry, who had a small income, her own car and a halfway decent apartment, and was as 'crazy' as I, supplementing her income by doing translations into her fluent French of scripts and art books. She even gave Paul McCartney the French words for one of the Beatles' top hit songs, translating them on the phone with her friend Peter Asher – brother of McCartney's girlfriend at the time Jane Asher. Carol worked holidays at Club Méditerranée hotels in Europe and loved nothing more than to go with me to concerts by Jimi Hendrix, Al Green, the Supremes and other Black American R&B stars performing in London.

There were Tricia and George, she with a comfortable private income and Sloane Street apartment; he, a fashionable advertising executive who looked exactly like John Lennon – to the delight of Italian restaurant maître d's.

There were friends who were actors or playwrights; gentle people, trendy, but not flashy, occasionally photographed in *Vogue* or *Queen* or *Harper's*, like cookery writer Adrian Routh and his wife, fashion designer May, who gave warm Sunday afternoon lunches of stews, salads and red wine, and mid-week dinner parties with a gourmet dish as centrepiece. All were a circle or two outside the high-level trendies, but not so much that the circles didn't overlap occasionally.

Restaurants were the usual places where these overlaps occurred, in a nice way. For instance, there was the Trattoria Terrazza, fondly known as 'The Trat', a downtown Soho Italian eating house with white, airy decor and great food, which was very fashionable. Its waiters were cheery to the point of familiarity, which was welcomed as a mark that you were a frequent customer. It was nice to hear your favourite waiter call out 'Signorina Barbara!' as you entered the restaurant with friends or, better still, clients you were taking to lunch.

The Trat was my favourite restaurant because their friendly welcome eased the shyness and fear I hid each time I had to take someone to lunch. I used to always order escargots (snails, if you don't know, and yes, they tasted very nice with garlic butter and hot French bread), scampi provençale with mashed potatoes to sop up the garlic tomato sauce, and spinach, that most delightful vegetable. I would finish with a slice of strawberry tart with cream, and never mixed business with pleasure.

The Trat became so fashionable that the Italian owners expanded their operation uptown to the middle of the King's Road at its most fashionable popularity, added a disco downstairs, and made the new restaurant a consistently sold-out eating place by making it a members' only club – the Aretusa. Everyone who was anyone went there at dinner time, and you were nobody unless you had been to the Aretusa.

People passing by on the crowded King's Road pavements could glimpse the true trendies of London flashing in and out of Rolls-Royces, paying their money just to be seen in the group they considered the top, and theirs.

The opening-night party was one of the best parties I ever went to, wall-to-wall film stars, models, artists, singers, famous and infamous people who lived in or passed through London. It was at the Aretusa that Tom Jones – then just beginning to be famous – winked at me across the dining room, and where I got invited to Sandie Shaw's birthday party being held at Madame Tussauds.

At the peak of the restaurant phase, Robin Sutherland, the accountant at Michael Rice & Co. who was one of my going-out friends, resigned and went into the restaurant business.

'Why?' I asked him.

'Because in a year's time I want to be driving my own Rolls-Royce,' he replied.

'No one drives their own Rolls-Royce,' I teased him.

But sure enough, he did it, partnering his Chinese best friend Michael Chow, who had style and artistic design ideas, in a series of elegant and fashionable Chinese restaurants – Mr Chow – the first of which was in Knightsbridge, but which now have expanded to be the most fashionable in New York and Los Angeles. Mr Chow carried the crowd from the other restaurants, including the Italian ones, whose high-energy waiters they hired. Its decor was ultra modern, clean lines, soft lighting and large black-and-white photos of celebrities on the walls. Indeed, what drew so many famous people to Mr Chow was to see their photo among the rest of the celebrities.

Yes, mine was there, dressed demurely in white.

(I had the last laugh on Robin, though, when he took me to a grand party on the stage of Sadler's Wells Opera to which I wore a full-length red velvet cloak over my evening dress. When the party was over, I waited outside on the pavement beside the costumed doorman, while Robin went for the Rolls-Royce. As he drove up and stopped before the entrance, the doorman stepped smartly up to the car . . . and opened the rear door for me to enter. 'I'll ride with the chauffeur,' I told him, opened the front door and got in, before collapsing into convulsions of laughter.)

Mr Chow imported chefs from Hong Kong – one to cook food, one to make pastry, one to make Peking duck, and one a master showman, who provided the popular entertainment of the evening by rolling out dough right in front of you and in a series of swift movements dividing it up into the finest angel-hair noodles possible in about five minutes. Fantastic!

The main Mr Chow gimmick, which set it apart from other

Chinese restaurants, was the Italian waiters who replaced the cool aloofness of the traditional Chinese waiters with their own brand of familiarity, efficiency and name-recognition. It was nice to be taken there on dates, or to be in a group with Robin and Michael, sitting near the kitchen door drinking white wine and eating nice things stirred up behind the swing doors for the delight of the owners' guests and watching the celebrities come and go.

After eating and drinking, we might all happily go on to a discotheque where we would drink more white wine and dance and chat to friends on the scene, even if there was work next day. Our pleasures were never taken to the excesses which might prevent us from working the following day, or even to interfere with tasks like taking the laundry to the laundromat on Saturday mornings. We left those excesses to the sybarites like Mick and Bianca, or John and Yoko or Twiggy and Vidal, whose lives did not include such ordinary duties.

Weekends were spent ambling along the Portobello Road examining the antiques – especially the vintage dresses from the thirties and forties which I loved to collect for their interesting fabrics, styles and bias-cut drapery – and buying the week's food on the half of the street which marked the boundary between the Black ghetto and the trendy homes. One could buy green bananas, yam, plantains, okras and sweet potatoes with which to stay in gastronomic touch with home.

Then a movie in the West End, or dinner, or best of all, a night of staying home bundled up watching three glorious colour channels of British television – the best. Friends might drop by on such a night and I would cook one of my famous French or Jamaican or Italian dishes and we'd eat over a bottle of wine and save all conversation for the commercial breaks.

Not a very 'Black' life, I can hear you criticize.

I agree totally.

But the thought that there was a Black alternative life did not occur to me. This was just 'life', and a young person enjoying it gently, doing the same things other young people did who weren't up to any trouble.

Sounds boring?

Arrogant?

Please, shhh, I pray you.

If any reader's judgements are so harsh, then I beg only patience to allow my humble story to unfold. My only arrogance perhaps, is to truly believe that the telling of my story can tear back even one veil off the eyes of my fellow Black people and allow us to stand, free and strong, and fulfil the great dream of our great Prophet and Leader, Marcus Mosiah Garvey, and our God.

The whole will soon be made clear and since I have been given the talent to write of my experience, stay with me.

My secretary Katerina was upper class too. As well as her salary she had 'an income', which meant that some relative or parent had put money in a trust which gave her a monthly allowance when arriving at a certain age. Certainly, she had more money than me, her boss, and it was she who turned me on to high-class clothes, Shetland sweaters, Jourdan shoes and French skirts.

But it was also she who asked me to translate into English the words of a pop record she had bought: '007 Shanty Town' by a Jamaican band I had never heard of, Desmond Dekker and the Aces. She was stumped by the Jamaican patois lyrics, and so was I. I couldn't translate them; I could hardly understand most of the words in the song myself!

'I thought you said you were Jamaican,' she joked.

We went to boutiques together. Each boutique had a designer and a particular style which was identifiable. Consciously and unconsciously, one had to project the right image through one's clothes. It was a subtle game played with money, and I joined in on as small a scale as my pocket would allow. I remember buying a soft shirt from Turnbull & Asser – THE leading British men's shirtmaker – and a one-of-a-kind leather skirt fringed like an American Indian, from Browns Boutique.

At the same time I took full advantage of the new fashion trend that the Flower Power era was creating. Clothes blossomed like flowers and we were free to be as outrageous as we wished. Clothes came from India, Morocco, Pakistan, Africa. Some girls painted their faces, frizzed their hair and wore bells. Carnaby Street became a Saturday promenade, where fashions for that night's discotheque were purchased and altered to fit on the spot.

I became a 'weekend hippie', hanging out at places which offered light and sound 'psychedelic' experiences at weekends.

Young White people began to show that even if their parents weren't being nice to Black people, they didn't share the same opinion. They acknowledged the Black influence in music and styles on their hippie culture, and welcomed us into their midst.

Among the Flower Power hippies, their minds expanded by the Eastern philosophy being explored by people like the Beatles, not to mention 'pot', I was happy and at home.

Clothes and fashion were central to the English sixties. Not to be left out, I did some charity modelling of Jamaican clothes under the crystal chandeliers of St James's Palace, for a VIP audience invited by Michael Rice. Though I did not mind the two or three times I did this (once with Bianca, the model who married Mick Jagger, and once with Shakira, the Miss Guyana who married Michael Caine), the thought of trying to make modelling a permanent feature of my life was never seriously considered, though I was often assumed to be a model because of my slim figure. All that such compliments gave me was a lessening of shame at my skinny legs; here at last was a country where my figure was envied, skinny legs and all.

I enjoyed working on the Jamaica PR account. Once I was a guest on a TV quiz show which I had persuaded to ask some questions on Jamaica. I remember the enormous bouquet of flowers they presented me with on camera. Mostly, I had to deal with requests from people wanting to go to Jamaica, or arrange for magazine coverage of Jamaica through press releases, or send editorial teams to Jamaica.

The high cost of a Jamaican vacation justified a campaign that was directed at the highest English circles, through the most high-class publications.

One such was a photo feature trip for *Queen* magazine, then the leading upper-class publication. Selected as photographer was an upcoming young man named Patrick Lichfield, whose hippie ways were in direct contrast to what was expected from an Earl and second cousin of Queen Elizabeth – which he was.

As it happened, the Kingston JTB office ordered me home on a familiarization trip, the dates of which overlapped with the 'Queen' visit and I spent some pleasant time in Montego Bay watching Patrick foil the attempts of the snobbish Mobay 'jet set' to separate his aristocratic company from me and the Tourist Board executive squiring him around, Deryck Roberts – both of whom he much preferred to be with. Lord Lichfield, they seemed to say, should be with White people, not bumming around with Jamaicans in an open-top Mini Moke.

We remained good friends after his trip, and it was fun to read of his playboy exploits later in the gossip columns when he used both his talent and title to earn a name and some fame for himself as a photographer, before settling down to a good marriage and respectability.

The trip home was a pleasant interlude. I spent a short time with my father, where I reaffirmed that I was not ready to come back home at all. My girlfriend Carol Martin-Sperry, who was visiting her father in Canada, flew down to join me for a week and we flew back to Montreal together to experience Expo '67, where I remember lining up for four and a half hours just to see a spectacular multi-screen film and light show by the National Film Board of Canada called *Labyrinth*. It was beautiful, and worth the wait.

Relationships followed the same predictable path. You met someone and thought you were in love. When it got boring after a while, that meant it wasn't love.

No one had taught a different way to conduct relationships.

The new philosophy of 'Make Love Not War' allowed for the freedom to have relationships that were conducted in this way. For some people, the relationship continued for a long time into a permanent union.

For others, it terminated.

Loving was natural and good.

In that manner, I gave some loving, if not love, to some fairly nice men. I was tricked out of some too, but mostly I received a good portion of that particular commodity, even though I may not have been aware of it at the time. One great love lasted two years, and there was a year of beautiful love and letters from architect Mike.

My life began to settle.

Among the people I met at parties were young radio programme producers, and I was often invited to be a panellist on programmes like *Petticoat Line*, where four women and a moderator would discuss letters sent in by listeners. I was expected to provide 'the young voice' as the regular panellists were older British women. There was the nice Scots woman, Renée, a faded Mae West type full of compassion and humour, who drank gin before the show to give her courage to deal with the provoking jibes of the programme's chairwoman who – for one reason or other – managed to depress Renée enough for her to cry before many shows, though she would bravely hide this and sweep away the show in her gutsy way to the cheers of the middle-aged audience.

I was the only Black person who ever took part in these shows, probably because I was the only Black person the producers had ever met who contained sufficient English-ness to be able to participate in these forms of entertainment. The panels usually featured a minor celebrity such as a young actress, a businesswoman, an authoress. Renée was always warm to me, and when one day she called me over and gave me a warm hug before a group of her fans who had stayed behind after the show ended, I realized that her embrace of me was a bold, defiant gesture to a group of people who could never contemplate having a Black friend.

What was it about my colour that they detested, like a horrible, contagious disease?

Could I never please these people?

How much more did they want me to be like them?

It was a kink they had in them before they ever met you, that they could never get rid of.

I also participated in a TV quiz show as a contestant, where I sat in Make-up watching the ageing hostess having her wrinkles wiped out by make-up skill, and was stupid enough to comment on the transformation.

'What kind of questions do you like, dear?' she asked, smiling with acid.

'English and General Knowledge,' replied the trusting me. She bowled me some Science and Geography, and bowled me right out of the studio and the prizes.

Around this time I met Vonetta McGee, a pale brown, beautiful American actress who was then living in Rome. We met at the

Aretusa on a foursome dinner date with sophisticated Jamaican Winston Stona and American journalist Jon Bradshaw. She was wearing short black shorts, black sweater and thigh-high black boots of Italian leather. I couldn't understand how anyone could be so beautiful and also such a nice person.

Everyone stared at her. I had no jealousy. It was simply astonishing just to be in her vibrant company and to learn, from observing her, how to let go of some of the tensions which inhibited me from being fully woman. That was in 1968, and each time since then that we met I never failed to learn something important just from the pleasure of being in her company. She remained a close girlfriend for many years after she became world famous from films like *Melinda* and *Shaft in Africa*.

In many ways we are like minds, but she is so confident of herself and men love her so instantly, that it took me a long time before I could stop feeling like a very much younger and more awkward little sister of hers. It also took three months of staying with her and her man Max Julien in Hollywood in 1973, and meeting such beautiful Black men as heavyweight boxer Ken Norton, for me to discover that – even next to Vonetta – I also had my own quiet, natural charms.

She came to London twice and stayed at my tiny Chepstow Road flat. My male flatmate David, who later got jailed for smuggling pot in Morocco, moved out and gave her his small room – anything for Vonetta, he agreed with total adulation. Another time she visited and we had adventures rushing around London, she doing as much shopping as she possibly could, me anxiously following in her wake.

On her second visit I took her to a Sunday party at John and Liz Pringle's, who had just set up London residence in what was certainly the most elegant home I had ever visited in my life. I also brought with us my friends Peter Cook (Dudley Moore's comic partner) and film-maker John Irvine who used to live and work in Jamaica. We all hung out on dark brown velvet cushions in their sunken den, drinking white wine and Scotch, enjoying good food cooked by Liz and served by their cap-and-aproned, smiling Jamaican maid. Vonetta laughingly fended off the men's inescapable admiration of her, all of us enjoying the company of people who were each someone in their own right, and enjoying life.

Around this time, too, I spent a lot of time smoking pot like everyone else did. Often, one got high in order to understand the hidden psychedelic meanings of the new Beatles songs, or to travel the Dylan trips, or to enjoy sitar music, light shows, pop music TV shows, underground newspapers, films and 'happenings'.

One such happening was the Stones concert in Hyde Park, the first major London gathering of hippies who, in a cool and calm manner, took over the whole of the giant and beautiful park on a cool, calm Saturday to pay homage to the high priests of rock and to identify with each other under the words Peace and Love. It was the first time so many hippies had gathered together in one place, and the throngs virtually took over the public transportation system of London to get to Hyde Park.

The vibrations and sights of that wonderful day can never be forgotten. Thousands of happy, carefree, smiling people wearing long skirts, caftans, bells, beads, sandals, long frizzed hair, face decorations, bare feet, bell-bottoms, jeans, hats, Indian feathers, bubbles and balloons. Over everything was a fragrant cloud of pot smoke, mingled with the smells of grass and trees, and over all that was the crazy music of the Rolling Stones. Near the end of the concert a thousand white pigeons were released to the skies, in a prayer for peace and the end of the Vietnam War, which showed the strength of the British alliance with the US anti-war movement. I was in heaven.

Times like these, as well as the Albert Hall concerts by Bob Dylan, Janis Joplin, Richie Havens, James Brown, Jimi Hendrix, Otis Redding and Eric Clapton, were like oases of pleasure whose memory we retained with languid evenings and nights in friendly company, listening to stereo music, watching the colour TV with the sound turned down, smoking pot and talking. It was a nice life, and I fervently subscribed to hippie values.

I couldn't bring my prim self to try acid, though. Something about how they described the total loss of mental control, made me scared that one trip would drive me mad, so I avoided it and was very suspicious of punches at parties which may have been spiked with acid.

I realize God really protected me at all times, because I can truthfully look back at England and say that I never did anything outrageous – no orgies or kinky sex and I can't remember ever being vindictive or spiteful. I just tried to live it properly, right, without even having a concept of what God was.

Such was my little life in London.

Into all this came a devilish, bitter-faced monster – a Conservative politician named Enoch Powell, previously unknown until he made a violently racist speech calling for an end to coloured immigration with the threat that, unless this occurred, England would flow with rivers of blood.

What really hurt about Powell's speech was how it enabled the racism, which seemed to be present in every older Briton, to come out from under the veneer of politeness and into the open. Almost overnight a new set of nasty, hostile actions and manners from White people towards Blacks were manifested.

The bus conductress who yesterday might simply have ignored you, today had some snarling sarcasm to hurl at you as she asked for your fare in a tone which implied that you did not intend to pay, or could not afford to.

The corner newsagent, who had for years refused to speak to you when you bought your daily paper and cigarettes, would today additionally keep you waiting for as long as possible while he conversed with another White person – sometimes even discussing in front of you what a nice person Enoch Powell was!

Schoolchildren would laugh together in groups and call out sentences with the word 'nigger' in them; women would spit on the street as you passed by. Articles in conservative publications became more racist; anti-immigrant stories, news items about trivial offences by Black people, or stories ridiculing 'immigrants', became popular. Exposés of the 'slums' we lived in were featured – none of them mentioning the fact that the only reason why we were allowed to live in the buildings in the first place was because they were well below decent standards. There were rehashes of the Christine Keeler–Lucky Gordon case, and endless stories about Black prostitution.

Powell's speech presented a counter-argument to the tolerance and love of humanity being preached by the younger generation, and made it legitimate for the British to display the racial hatred that they had been taught since the seventeenth-century beginning of slavery.

Yes, the seventeenth century – for it was only by describing the African as a savage animal . . . not human . . . not equal to the White . . . inferior in civilization, learning and brain capacity . . . fit only to be beast of burden and sex object for their basest desires . . . it was only thus that the White race could justify their brutalization and enslavement of the Black.

The golliwogs . . . Little Black Sambo stories . . . Tarzan movies . . . these formed the basis of the English view of Africa, the Dark Continent, and caused a natural resentment among White people at finding themselves forced to live side by side with a race they had been taught to despise as inferiors. Since living among Blacks must surely have demonstrated that deep down Blacks were little different from Whites, this contradiction between propaganda and reality must have been a bitter pill for many Whites to swallow, and many refused to let go of their prejudices. Enoch Powell became a spokesman and hero to these Whites.

At the heart of much White resentment against Blacks was interracial relationships. The British hated to see mixed couples and mixed-race children – though White men assumed, as I have said, that all Black women were freely available to them.

I, too, hated to see a Black man with a White woman, for it

showed me that the man didn't want me. I was used to this rejection by Black men in favour of White women, but at that time I felt no scorn for the Black man but instead a greater sense of inferiority at my inability to come up to the White ideal which every Black man seemed to desire.

The British feared that more coloured children in their schools would mean more interracial sex and marriage, and they preferred the purity of their race.

Why not?

The issue of coloured immigration became so heated that a decision was finally taken to debate the matter in Parliament. I had never been to the House of Commons, but for some reason I wanted to be there, for some reason I wanted my 'coloured' presence to be seen as proof that we existed, that we were no threat, that we only wanted to live and let live. I found out who my MP was – a Conservative – and obtained a ticket for the debate.

I took a bus and as it drew near Whitehall, an enormous traffic jam halted us. I got off and walked through what I later learned was a massive anti-immigrant demonstration by London dock workers – a group noted for their racist attitudes and employment policies. I later read that the dockers spat on the ambassadors of Kenya and India as they entered the British Houses of Parliament. For some reason, they only stared at me as, dressed in a brown wool Jaeger suit, brown Charles Jourdan boots and a hat, I made my way through the throng to take my seat in the Public Gallery.

I didn't stay for the entire debate. Apart from not understanding what was going on, I was shivered by the fact that two

MPs – total strangers – sent notes up to my seat inviting me to meet them for dates. On each occasion as the note was delivered and I read it, I looked down into the sea of faces to see a lecherous pink face leering up at me.

My own MP, however, I admired enough to later campaign for in our Notting Hill constituency, especially as he and his wife had adopted a near-blind mixed-race baby. They went to great trouble to befriend me, especially to show that not all Conservatives shared Powell's racist views. My MP was only one of a handful of pro-coloured MPs on both sides who opposed the swell of pro-Powell parliamentarians. He was fighting a losing battle, but he knew he was right. The opposing Labour candidate campaigned in our predominantly Black neighbourhood in a red sports car on which sat two mini-skirted blondes – he didn't appeal at all.

The Conservative won.

Chapter Nine

When 'The Break' came, it was so unexpected I didn't even have time to realize that something important was happening to me. Becoming 'the first Black woman journalist on British television', as I was referred to, happened like this.

After three years at Michael Rice, I began to feel restless. The Jamaica account had become repetitive, especially since the Kingston head office was extremely conservative. The only stories I was allowed to encourage (this was 1967/1968) had to be centred around the 'jet set', that unreal world of rich White people totally unknown to Jamaicans whose wealth enabled them to holiday in their expensive, high-walled Montego Bay or Ocho Rios winter palaces, complete with maids, chauffeurs and gardeners. Such was the clientele of Jamaican tourism at that time and the natives had been well trained to be excellent servants in this modern-day plantocracy.

I once dared to suggest a photo-spread on the Rastafarians (those colourful people, I explained, not knowing much more at the time). Head Office was horrified! The only non-slave natives allowed to be featured in the kind of article Head Office cultivated were the White upper-class Jamaicans and those Blacks who had so successfully copied the White lifestyle to be eligible for membership among that elite.

I had been lucky to get a visit to Denmark, Norway, Sweden and Finland on a wintertime JTB promotional tour with a limbo dancer, fire-eater, policeman and a calypso band (that was what the JTB presented as typical entertainment offered in Jamaican hotels). Scandinavia was a great experience for me, a snow-covered set of four totally different countries. My father's third wife was Danish and, as our stepmother from when I was ten till sixteen, I had learned a lot about that country and it was nice to see it in real life. Norway, my favourite of the four Scandinavian countries, had the warmest people, my first sight of a ski jump and great open sandwiches.

In Sweden the most handsome White man I ever saw, a Swedish-Hungarian Count, saw me at our JTB press conference and was smitten with me. He was tall and slim, with jet black hair and very blue eyes, and for the three days we were in Stockholm he followed me around, invited me to sail on his yacht, and when I declined, he offered to sail it from Stockholm to meet me in Copenhagen. He was charming, but I was working and maintained an on-the-job demeanour to decline his invitation.

On the group's final evening, the entertainers performed at the grand nightclub of the hotel at which we stayed overlooking the city, and at which famed Black British singer Shirley Bassey was to headline after our Jamaican cultural show. The star lady came to sit at our table after the Jamaican show, but it soon became embarrassingly obvious that she was there only to show her attraction to the handsome Count. But despite her fame, wealth and beauty the gentleman still only had eyes for me. I was flattered by this beautiful man's tender attention, and seeing him spurn such a famous lady did a lot to boost my self-esteem, but I could not envisage myself as a Swedish Countess. He called me later in London, and even came to visit, but I felt no warmth for him, alas.

I was enjoying the job but I wasn't moving, except in circles, on the job. So I looked around for another.

As part of my job, I had finally managed to get an article published in the prestigious *Sunday Times Magazine* by offering them a feature on Jamaican food for a series on world cuisine. They agreed, on condition that I cook the dishes for them, so I appeared in full colour with a photo of me dressed in bandana costume, sitting proudly behind dishes of ackee and saltfish, boiled green bananas and coconut cream pie all cooked by yours truly. Not only did I get featured; I also got paid. Best of all, I also got entry into British journalism through the most elite door, beginning a journalistic friendship with the *Sunday Times* which continued until I left England.

When I read in the papers that two new London-based independent television networks were shortly to begin operating, I wrote to each enclosing my article and asking for work as a writer. One of them, Thames Television, replied asking me to come for an interview.

I met a tall, greying Scotsman named Alex Valentine, who

asked me questions about my career and then asked me to come back and do an audition, explaining that perhaps writers would occasionally have to present their stories. The proposed programme was a daily magazine show, to be aired between six and six-thirty weekdays over Greater London. I envisaged a sort of freelance arrangement.

I arrived for the audition not expecting any big deal. In a room were seven or eight other people. I was given a paper which instructed me that I should write a news story on one of five listed topics. Then I would have to read some news from the teleprompter, a machine fixed above the camera lens on which the printed script unrolls as you read. Then I would interview the 'leader of a White mercenary unit fighting in Africa, whose rank of "colonel" was self-assumed and who was in fact being paid to defend multinational interests in the Nigerian civil war, even if this meant killing Africans'.

I composed my thoughts, then chose as my topic a story about a woman celebrating her 100th birthday. Recalling the pattern of such stories on British TV, I worked out how many wars, coronations and modern inventions she would have been alive to experience, gave her a large number of children, grandchildren and great-grandchildren, and then added a funny ending.

'When asked the secret of her longevity,' I wrote, 'she replied: "I never bathed much . . . a little dirt never hurt anyone, unless it fell on them." '

I then committed the story to memory; an ability which turned out to be an asset for television journalism. I was neither afraid nor apprehensive, for I had worked with JBC-TV before I left home as a contestant then later as a hostess of a quiz game show, and had twice experienced British TV studios, so the audition was no big thing. As far as I knew, this was a mere formality to my getting a writing job for which I knew I was qualified. I could not have dreamed that I was actually auditioning for a full-time on-camera job.

I stood before the camera and delivered my story on the hundred-year-old woman. On the final sentence, the studio crew laughed, so that was alright.

I was given a run-through with the teleprompter, and saw at once that the story included French and Spanish place names as part of the test. I smiled, inwardly pleased at my French and Spanish knowledge, and then read it through with careful attention to the foreign pronunciations.

Then I was taken to a set with two chairs and a table, where I was introduced to 'Colonel X'. It was not difficult to interview him, though the actor playing him had been well briefed. I don't remember my exact questions. I certainly cannot claim that I had even one shred of 'Black awareness', but even knowing it was an actor under instruction I still felt hostile to this character and his motives for being in Africa.

I asked about the circumstances under which he obtained his commission and, when he could not be specific, thereafter addressed him as 'Mister'. I asked him whether, since he said he was fighting on behalf of Africa, his unit included any Africans, and he said it didn't because he did not think Black and White could or should mix. Could he then be said to be protecting British interests? I asked.

Yes.

How then could he be against Black and White mixing, if he wanted the White to remain in the Black man's country? He couldn't answer that either.

The research information given me indicated that this man was to be exposed, and as politely as I could, I made it easy for all to see from his answers that he was no more than a callous and unscrupulous mercenary.

I was told later that when I finished my audition, there was applause in the control room where the production team was viewing it. I, however, knew nothing of this. Hoping I had got some freelance work, I returned to the office and prepared to continue my search for full-time employment.

Three weeks later Alex Valentine called me and asked me to have lunch with him. Over Italian food, he asked if I would like to work as a TV reporter on his programme.

I was astonished!

Work in television!

On screen!

Why not, I thought.

It's a job.

In his half-joking, half-serious way, Alex advised me: 'Be nice to the people you meet on the way up, for you're sure to meet them on the way down.' He was giving me notice that I was about to climb the ladder of stardom, but I had not a clue what to expect.

I later discovered that 300 people had been auditioned, and that I had been the first of three offered the job.

There was only one condition.

'You have to cut your hair,' Alex said.

It was shoulder length and I was proud of it.

'Why?'

'We think it would be better,' was all he replied.

For a person like me, constantly changing hairstyles, it did not really matter. But later, with a short haircut for the first time since I had my first cold-straightening, I learned that the reason was that the other girl chosen to join me as a reporter, an English actress named Jane Probyn, had shoulder-length hair also and it was preferred, for some reason, that we both shouldn't have the same hair style. I would have to sacrifice mine.

I consented.

It was a small detail, yet part of the delicate, spider-like web of racism which was, even then, being woven around me.

Not that I noticed the web.

The first alarm came when the station called a press conference to introduce the three reporters (there was also a man named Allan Hargreaves) and the programme's star, Eamonn Andrews the host of *This Is Your Life*. Not until the following day's papers appeared did I realize that the reason for the hurried exit of most of the reporters as we entered was that they had rushed back to write the scoop-making news that one of the reporters was a Black girl. I posed contentedly with the others for publicity photos, not realizing that my colour had yanked me from the comfortable haven of obscurity and made me a national celebrity.

The story of Britain's first Black daily TV reporter made the front page of every newspaper in London, some carrying photos, though not the *Daily Express,* noted for its pledge never to print a Black face on its front page 'so as not to upset the readers' breakfasts', it was said. The *Express* headline simply read, 'The Other BB', making a sexual association with then-sex-symbol, French actress Brigitte 'BB' Bardot!

There were other articles, too, all of which always made me ask myself: Did I really say that?

Here I am, the proper, integrationist 1968 Barbara Blake: 'Professional people like myself from the West Indies, India or Pakistan fit into similar jobs in Britain without too much trouble . . .' That excerpt from an article which begins: 'If anyone asks me again what it's like to be London's first coloured television reporter, I'm going to punch them . . .' (*TV Times*).

'My Lovely First Week' (*Sunday Mirror*): 'Already one racist has sent the company an obscene letter about her. But Barbara, daughter of a magazine editor and novelist, doesn't give a hoot. She promptly suggested to her boss, producer Alex Valentine, that the funniest ones received should be stuck up on a board for a giggle. Otherwise,' the article continued, 'my lovely first week had been "simply marvellous", she says with her cool, engaging smile, which I venture will captivate millions.'

Really!

A racist letter already!

And was I really so cool about it?

I know it worried me enough to make me serious.

What was it about these people that made them hate you so much?

I hadn't done them anything.

At least I was serious enough to say, in the Thames TV PR handout: '"Tomorrow the world? Good Lord, no!" she said. "If I have one ambition, it's to become the world's best cook. I love cooking, it's the most immediate way to please people. I suppose French cooking is my speciality, not Jamaican because it takes so long. I only cook Jamaican for very close friends."'

After four years in London, does she regard it as home?

'Not really. I shall go back to Jamaica and settle. Jamaica has changed since Independence. For one thing, our culture, which was buried for a long time under the British, is developing at a rapid rate and I find this very exciting. I guess I am still national-istic at heart.'

Chapter Ten

Christopher Columbus discovered Jamaica in 1494. What a nice man he was to do that. If he hadn't discovered Jamaica, we would have remained lost and forgotten, an invisible land without modern civilized amenities, without our English language and Queen; a total zero. What a lovely man was Christopher Columbus, to discover us.

Henry Morgan was the boldest and bravest and richest pirate of all, and we are lucky that he made Jamaica his headquarters because that is one of Jamaica's claims to fame. He was such a good pirate that the Queen of England knighted him and made him Governor of Jamaica. At one time Jamaica's Port Royal was the richest city in the world, thanks to the wealth of people like Henry Morgan.

The African came to Jamaica as a slave, and even though slavery was a bad thing, at least the slave was taught to wear clothes and speak English and learn the Bible. If the African hadn't been brought to Jamaica, we would still be living in trees in the jungle in Africa, eating people and speaking 'ugga, ugga' like the savages in the Tarzan movies. Nowadays the African is part of the great British Empire which won the Second World War, and those who are not too Black and speak English properly stand a good chance of rising to the top and being a success in the Mother Country.

The Lake District is . . .

The average mean rainfall of the British Isles is . . .

The elm and ash and oak trees of Great Britain are . . .

I wandered lonely as a cloud that floats on high o'er vales and . . .

To be or not to be Black is not a choice which can be made by a person fed on a steady diet of the above information which passed as learning and socialization in the schoolrooms and living rooms of the Jamaican fifties, sixties and – sadness – the seventies. Marcus Garvey, where were you?

A more accurate version of the above statements would be: the tides of human history cause sweeping changes when the civilizations of peoples are touched by the more aggressive and greedy peoples. Thus it was that the lives of the gentle Arawak Indians were invaded by pale-skinned peoples who arrived on Jamaican shores in wooden boats, and whom the innocent, loving Indians welcomed with the hospitality they assumed they would receive in similar circumstances.

These pale-skinned immigrants, with whom there was a language barrier, soon demonstrated with the language of brutality that their interests were material and fleshy, and when the rape of gold ornaments and golden bodies was over, all that remained were diseased natives dying of VD, and a beautiful tropical island that resembled Paradise.

Material greed and violence were not the prerequisites of the Spanish people only, and just like the colonists of Portugal, France, Denmark and Germany, the British demonstrated in Jamaica that these were characteristics which ran through the Caucasian race as a whole in their relations with African people. Perhaps the best example of these horrible excesses lay in the person of the bloodthirsty pirate Henry Morgan, who ruled at the head of a band of men whose occupation was the looting and plunder of the many ships that carried slavery's booty through the sea lanes of the Caribbean.

Morgan and his co-workers made Port Royal their headquarters, until God intervened by way of an earthquake that sank two-thirds of this city of murderers and thieves to the bottom of Kingston Harbour. Undaunted by this divine message, England felt it appropriate to name Morgan Governor of Jamaica, a clear indication of the English value system.

Into an Africa ravaged by sixteenth-century wars, came the Europeans seeking labourers for their newly acquired colonial properties. Using their also newly acquired gunpowder, they were soon able to institute an export in captured Africans to the Americas and a slavery unparalleled in savagery, brutality and genocide.

Justifying the trade by quoting the traditional, but far more benign, barter of people which had existed for years among the Northern African Arab tribes, the Europeans were also assisted in their foul deeds by Africans who wished to punish their vanquished foes, and Africans who, out of self-interest, allied their services to the power and wealth of the Europeans and assisted in the enslavement of their brothers and sisters.

Nevertheless, these African traitors received relative pittances as pay for their misdeeds and, sooner or later, found themselves captured and enslaved by the same Europeans they helped. To be sure, no fortunes were made by the Africans in the slave trade, but this has not stopped this type of paid traitor from existing even today.

The brutality of the Middle Passage, where cultured and civilized Africans were packed like rats in the slime of human excrement, disease and rotting bodies, was exceeded only by the physical and psychological brutality of slavery on Caribbean plantations. Those ignorant of the real horrors of slavery often wonder why Africans seemed to offer little resistance to it, although they outnumbered the Whites on every plantation. This apparent non-resistance is often at the root of many a Negro's scorn of his own Black ancestors.

But the story has not been fully told of the excessive punishments that were meted out to dampen the will to resist, whenever a spark of independence or zest for freedom stirred in the enslaved breast. Pregnant women were strung up and their bellies slit open for the unborn child to drop at the feet of the forcibly assembled slaves. Beautiful Black warriors were castrated slowly before similar audiences. Children were maimed and mutilated, to say nothing of the tactics of separation of families and loved ones. Though it was a constant battle, the liberation of the African slave from physical bondage took 300 years. Psychologically, the struggle continues.

I had no awareness of the real version of my history. Armed with my English colonial education in the location of the Lake

District, the average mean rainfall of the British Isles and other equally irrelevant information, plus – thankfully – the wonderful education that comes from reading any and everything, I was well equipped to enter into this new phase of my life in the Mother Country.

It was not then necessary to know of the existence of a man named Marcus Garvey. That sweet revelation was reserved for later.

The job itself was really nice and lots of fun. It was great to have a job where I was doing something different every day. I would come to work at 8.30 each morning and either be sent out on a story with a film crew or told who I would be interviewing in the studio that evening. I would be given the background information and time to do my own follow-up calls or search the library for more facts from newspapers or clippings on which to base my questions.

The interview might be recorded or live, in which case I would have to go to Make-Up to be primped and have my hair groomed before going on set. By that time I was supposed to have thought out my questions and how I would ask them to obtain the answers the story needed. I would gauge the talk for the length of time allocated and prepare a lead-in and closing statement. Sometimes these were scripted by the producers or one of the programme's six researchers, but my questions were my own and it was my responsibility to ask them in a way that fully aired the topic under discussion.

We were given no lessons. I just did what I thought I ought to do. Some three weeks after the station and programme started broadcasting, some of the workers went on strike and closed down the studio to demand better pay. During this time we reporters, who were not of the same union, had to come in to work. This was when we first met Jeremy Isaacs, then the Thames current affairs producer responsible for our programmes, among others. He was a brilliant TV producer with a reputation for documentaries that exposed serious issues.

He called us to his office daily and gave us some basic lessons in how to conduct our interviews, especially in the technique of phrasing a question so as not to get a simple 'Yes' or 'No' answer, but a whole answer. I found him the nicest, most genuine person at Thames, with a real concern that we should be journalists, not merely TV celebrities. He and his wife remained my friends long after I left the programme.

The other people on the show were: host Eamonn Andrews, a TV celebrity for the past ten years first as a boxing commentator, then as host of Britain's number one show *This Is Your Life*. Eamonn was Irish and lost no time telling me on my first day that he had a Jamaican in-law by marriage and had visited the island on holiday. Though the Jamaican relative was a wealthy 'browning', I understood that he was letting me know in his gentle Irish way that he had no prejudices whatsoever. In the times we were living in, good people often made a point of showing you right away that they had no racial prejudices. I'll never forget the Christmas present he gave me – an entire side of smoked salmon, a very expensive and luxurious treat indeed.

Eamonn hosted the show and conducted the day's major interview. As he was not a journalist, his main questions were scripted, but he had enough natural personality and intelligence to make the interviews relaxed and interesting.

Jane Probyn was a beautiful would-be actress with a deep voice that was surprising in such a little person. She also was not a journalist but hired for her looks and personality and so relied a lot on researchers to help with her questions. Being the first show of its kind, *Today* had been created to a formula and since there were few young female journalists at that time with camera experience, the ability to relate to a television camera was considered more important than being able to write a good story. There was always the researcher to do the journalistic leg work.

This tactic of choosing pretty faces for television journalism still operates today and I think it was my good luck that I happened to combine a modest amount of both qualities.

The male reporter was Allan Hargreaves, a tall and rather camp, but lovable man who had spent his last few years working with a radio station in Malta. He was very affectionate, fussy about his work, and always asking anxiously if he was doing a good job. His approach must have been the correct one, for he kept the job for ten years.

Then there was an assortment of about seven researchers, young men and women with ambitions to be Fleet Street journalists or TV producers, whose job it was to search the newspapers and their contacts to find suitable stories for the programme.

Often the public, celebrity agents, publicists or people of importance would ring the office with a story item, and it was the job of the researchers to do the initial vetting for suitability, go out and meet with people, travel to inspect story venues and report to camera crews and reporters. Often they would work with us in the editing rooms, helping to put a story together because the reporter was busy elsewhere when editing time came. They were hardworking, and the backbone of the show.

One of them, Christine, became a flatmate and remained my friend for years after. Two others, David, who got busted in Morocco, and Martin, who went to live in Canada, shared my Chepstow Road flat for a while.

Then there were two programme directors, who took turns to be in charge of the studio shows and the film units. They had the final say on everything about the show. One was Alex Valentine, the nicely crazy Scotsman about whom I've already told you. The other was a woman whose name I genuinely forget. She was a plump, middle-aged person who seemed to have a fetish about being untidy and could well have been going through her change-of-life crisis, while the office constantly rang with rumours about the tragic course of her love life. She did not exude much warmth towards me, which I interpreted as caused by the fact that I had a better relationship with Alex Valentine, while she was engaged in a power struggle against him.

My first assignment was to report on a murder that had taken place the evening before in Tower Hill, a White working-class area near the Tower of London. While I waited for the 'OB unit' (I had no idea what that was), I tried to get some details from the police station and the pub which had been the scene of the incident. I was all alone and felt very Black indeed.

But surprisingly, because I could introduce myself as being from a TV programme, racial hostilities were temporarily suspended. Eventually, after a two-hour wait, three large trucks from the Outside Broadcast unit rolled up and out of them were unloaded TV cameras linked to a small broadcasting link located in one of the trucks.

The third vehicle contained the crew and my story's director. I briefed him on the information I had obtained, the people I was going to interview and, when the cameras were set up, I spoke my introduction to camera, conducted the interviews, 'wrapped up' with my end statement, and my first story was over.

Back at the Thames studios I watched the first programme with my story in the hospitality 'Green Room', where programme guests and workers could view a TV monitor while sipping drinks before, during and after the broadcast.

I started learning how to be a television interviewer right on the job. The first part was easy: feeling at ease before the camera, whether looking directly into it to deliver an introduction, or ignoring it completely as it watched the interview and sent out pictures back to the control room to be transmitted over the London region.

My second story was to cover the giveaway of items from the Beatles' Apple store. Fame and fortune had led the Beatles to diversify their empire and they had opened a store selling hippie clothes and other items on Baker Street, an area of tepid gentility with pretensions of aristocracy which was especially famous as the home of fictional hero Sherlock Holmes. The Beatles' store was on a corner and residents had objected to the fact that they had repainted the two sides of the three-storey building with a mural in the typical colourful fashion and imagery of the Flower Power generation.

Reds and blues and greens and yellows and purples swirled over each other on the building's walls. Gods and goddesses with flowers in their hair lay intertwined in dreamy bliss. The whole mural gave off an air of abandon and psychedelic drugs, and as the corner became a special visiting spot for hippies and members of Swinging London, the store became extremely popular.

Outraged at this invasion of their 'respectable' neighbourhood, the residents' objections led to a civic order for the Beatles to remove the offending mural. They responded in typical irreverent Beatles fashion, by announcing that they were not only going to close down the store, but would be giving away every single thing in it!

As can be imagined, the day of the giveaway was a moment of total hysteria in London. Baker Street was blocked for its entire length with thousands of people, hippies and otherwise, trying to jam their way in to get something free. I am sure the Beatles hoped that at least a few of the objecting residents had heart attacks on witnessing the scene of this triumphant contempt of material and social values.

It took me over an hour to get into the shop, and I only achieved this with the assistance of a policeman whom I managed to convince that I was from the *Today* programme and *had* to meet my film crew inside. I managed to get not only my story, but also a beautiful long wild silk scarf. Some people got leather suits, suede boots, chiffon dresses and Beatles records.

Every day presented some different story and location, taking me all over inner and outer London, meeting a variety of people: bus conductors, politicians, children, celebrities, priests, protestors. You name them, I met them.

One interview I remember took place on Chelsea Bridge with some British and American Hell's Angels who had been brought to London by John Lennon. Also there were Ken Kesey the hippie leader, a couple of members of the Grateful Dead and people from Apple, the Beatles' music company. I interviewed the British Hell's Angel, Mitch Mitchell, who was there with his band the Wild Angels who had just played a gig at the Albert Hall for Swinging London's top dress designers Ossie Clark and Alice Pollock, who had hired the venue for a party.

I did my usual work on what I considered the usual kind of interview, but later one of the research assistants who arranged the story confessed one-on-one to me that the story they had hoped to get was one of confrontation between the notoriously racist Hell's Angels and my Black self. Unfortunately, nothing of the sort happened and the interview fizzled out like a damp squib.

Of all the famous people I interviewed, the nicest was Jack Benny, the American comedian. The programme producers decided that both Jane and I should interview him, and he enjoyed being in the company of two pretty women, laughing and joking during the entire interview and making it more of an entertainment for viewers than a serious conversation. He came back to London a few months later for a charity show, and sent special invitations to Jane and me, sitting us on each side of him for the party which followed.

I interviewed Sir Francis Chichester, the first man to sail solo around the world. I did a rather nauseating interview on the day of the opening of the oyster season with a man whose cat ate oysters. I interviewed Michael Caine and his girlfriend at the time, Bianca, who later married Mick Jagger, when both were raising funds for child refugees of the Vietnam War.

I did interviews with poor Whites complaining of bad housing, and for the first time saw the horrors of British housing poverty; mildewed, stinking horror chambers where six or seven lived in one room on welfare. I interviewed residents of council tower blocks, where living twenty storeys above the ground was causing serious psychological problems among residents, including juvenile crime and housewife drug addiction.

I was given the assignment to interview the Caribbean leaders attending the Commonwealth Conference in London, but Hugh Shearer who was Jamaica's Prime Minister at the time wouldn't let me interview him, saying it was his first Conference and he just wanted to be an observer.

Some excuse.

Someone else who wouldn't let me interview him was Michael X, the infamous Trinidadian Michael de Freitas who, at the height of the fame of Malcolm X, announced in the British press that he had formed an organization with the initials RAAS on behalf of Britain's coloured people. West Indians, especially Jamaicans who knew that the word was the baddest Jamaican cuss word, couldn't believe the seriousness with which the British press accepted Michael X.

The Black community knew him well as a pimp and chief

enforcer for Rachman, the Notting Hill ghetto's worst slum lord, who used terror tactics of dogs, beatings and killings to collect rent from West Indian immigrants. We cringed with shame at the thought that he pretended to represent us. But in the climate of racial hostility engendered by Enoch Powell, the press was happy to have a Black extremist to match the White one.

The press lost no time in letting the world know that this presumed champion of the Black race was also an associate of Lucky Gordon, the Jamaican pimp of notorious Christine Keeler, the alleged English prostitute whose relationship with a British Cabinet Minister and a Russian diplomat caused a scandal that brought down the Conservative government of the time.

But his criminal links were an asset at that time for Black leaders. Black Power was just beginning to be heard of. Tommie Smith had raised a black-gloved fist at the Mexico Olympics. Angela Davis had become the Most Wanted Woman in America. Malcolm X, Eldridge Cleaver, Rap Brown and Huey Newton had, in writings and speeches, begun to demonstrate that Blacks who had been through the American prison system were prepared to use their badness to confront and smash racism. Michael de Freitas's criminal background was seen as his best credential for leading the British struggle.

One day I learned that the West Indians of Notting Hill and Ladbroke Grove had organized a carnival parade through the streets of our depressed neighbourhood. I used a lot of persuasion to get the programme's producers to schedule coverage of the parade, for they were very reluctant to do a story in our ghetto and it was taking place on a Sunday. But they agreed, and we found ourselves on a drizzly Sunday filming what became the first Notting Hill Carnival. It was a fairly lacklustre event, one steel band, a car with music and a few hundred Black revellers hoping to recapture the laughter and gaiety of our homeland holidays.

Suddenly I glimpsed a face in the crowd that I recognized from newspaper photos as Michael X. I went up to him with my microphone seeking a comment on camera, but he refused to speak to me, turning and walking away rudely while insulting me for being in the company of White people. I shrugged off my annoyance and embarrassment.

But a few weeks later I was surprised to meet this ghetto champion of the Black race surrounded by White people at a party in the home of my friend Feliks Topolski, a top society artist and friend of the Queen's sister Princess Margaret. I was eating some grapes when Michael X came over and asked sardonically: 'You want me to peel that grape for you?'

Not yet knowing that de Freitas survived on the largesse of society people such as those at this upper-class party, I asked him why he had refused to let me interview him at the Carnival, yet was now in the company of the very Whites he claimed to scorn.

'Because you don't have a Jamaican accent,' he replied.

I was furious.

'How are you different from the people who won't let me interview them because I don't have a White skin?' I asked him. 'You are just as racist as they are,' and I walked away from him, proud of the fact that, whether I spoke with an English accent or not, my efforts had given the Notting Hill community the first ever positive exposure on British TV.

I bumped into Michael X at a few similar social occasions, but I avoided any further contact. Soon stories began to circulate in the ghetto about him using the same strong-arm landlord tactics to raise money to finance his bid for political power, and I was not in the least surprised to read of his final end in Trinidad, accused of the murder of one of the London society people who got their kicks from associating with such dangerous company.

Another story which I remember covering was the Russian invasion of Czechoslovakia, my assignment being simply to stand outside the Russian Embassy all day reporting on the comings and goings in and out of the Embassy gates. I was not familiar with the background to the story and the international importance of the invasion and was getting very nervous about making a live introduction to camera at the 6.05 p.m. start of the show.

However, I remember being completely reassured watching a senior reporter from the independent news channel ITN, who was using our OB unit to broadcast a 6 p.m. news story, deliver his story with knees trembling so hard he seemed about to collapse. Thankful that TV cameras hardly ever showed reporters below the waist, I was silently relieved at this evidence that 'butterflies in the stomach' were not restricted solely to novices like myself.

In fact, though, I was hardly ever nervous. I found the job of TV interviewing the easiest work I have ever done. I love meeting people and asking them about themselves, and to be paid to do this was wonderful.

Perhaps this is why I didn't let the fact of being a minor celebrity go to my head, for my habits didn't change in any way from what they had been when I worked with Michael Rice. After a day's work I took a taxi home, cooked dinner, set my hair in rollers and watched TV until it was time to go to bed and prepare for another day's work. In fact, my desire to treat the job just like any other job must have been frustrating for my agent, a young woman in London's top celebrity agency, who also handled David Frost who was just beginning his own career as a TV journalist after success as a satirist in the new crop of British TV comedy shows.

An agent was someone who negotiated the best possible contract and salary for you, and tried to arrange other deals which earned you income in any number of ways, taking a percentage of what you earned. An agent would try to arrange special appearances on other TV shows, at charity events, endorsing products, commercials, articles and books.

My services were not at all in demand for any of these lucrative opportunities, since I was not an entertainer or model, but rather simply a journalist who worked in the TV medium. I didn't help matters much by not behaving in a star-like manner. With hindsight, I wish I had had enough self-confidence (and perhaps the help of a good partner) to cash in on my uniqueness. As it was, I simply resisted doing anything except being a journalist, and hopefully a good one. No regrets, really, except financial ones especially when my pocket grew empty.

After about six months, problems started emerging between the two producers. Alex was a journalist, and wanted a news magazine programme. The plump female was more in favour of making the programme a patchwork of cute, trivial items. There was therefore a power struggle going on. To her mind the show had one producer too many, and her conspiracy was assisted by two of the female researchers. Alex, no conspirator, simply got on with the business of producing a lively and interesting show.

Allan, Jane and I had each been given contracts to run for nine months initially, with options for renewal. Mine, having been the first signed, was the first to come up for renewal. As this time approached, my agent started negotiating. At this time also, something unpleasant started happening.

I knew that the programme often received 'hate mail' from racists objecting to a Black person being on their television screens. Alex and I had even joked that we would put the funniest ones up on the notice board, though we never did. But it was only on the rare occasions when a phone call came through growling racist obscenities and threats that I would realize that not only were my calls screened, but much of the hate mail was being kept out of my sight. I silently thanked Alex for this.

Once when a phone call was put through to me, and I listened silently to a racist, then quietly put the phone down, I noticed that everyone in the open office was looking at me, and I knew that they knew what the phone call was about and were watching to see my reaction. I just continued working as if nothing had happened.

Suddenly the hate mail became visible. A letter would be left lying casually on a desk. Several more phone calls were put through to me. Finally, one special day, I was called into the woman producer's office, on whose desk was arranged a showcase display of the best of the hate letters. 'Get that nigger off our television. Can't you find a decent White girl? Otherwise we will bomb you, nigger-lover.'

That was the gist of most of it. The producer talked to me, not about the letters that we both could clearly see before us, but about some trivial item about the story I was working on.

The next day, as I stood on a genuinely freezing country road-side to do a story about motorists causing accidents by driving too fast, Christine, who was the story's researcher, told me that she didn't want to tell me, but unless I did a really good report on that story, my contract wasn't going to be renewed.

As I interviewed a man whose jaws were wired shut and whose face bore bloody evidence that he was a recent victim of one of the many accidents on that strip of road, as I talked with the local councillor on the subject and tried to stamp some circulation into my numb feet, I wondered what more I could inject into my inter-viewing that had not already been demonstrated in the past nine months. I couldn't find an answer.

I returned to the studio and appealed to Jeremy Isaacs.

Yes, he was in charge.

Yes, he thought I was doing a good job, but he couldn't force a producer to keep a performer she didn't want.

Yes. She.

Alex, the professional, had been dismissed.

Allan's contract was extended for six months, Jane's for another three (at the end of which it was not renewed). In my place the producer hired Sandra Harris, a blonde, blue-eyed Australian.

I was out of work.

The *Sketch* newspaper wrote: 'Eamonn's Show Drops Its

139

Coloured Reporter. Barbara Blake, Britain's first coloured girl TV interviewer, is leaving the Eamonn Andrews ITV magazine *Today*. Last night a spokesman for Thames Television, the London weekday station which screens the show, said, "We have not renewed her contract. She did not fit into the format of the programme." When she was chosen for the show, Thames denied that her selection was to cater for West Indian viewers. An official explained: "She is a very good interviewer and that's it." Last night Miss Blake said: "I'd rather not discuss this. I'll be going home to Jamaica soon for a short holiday, but I have work lined up as a freelance with BBC radio." '

You know, I have met so many Jamaicans since that time who tell me what a wonderful job I did and how glad they are to meet me because of how proud I made them feel to see me on their television doing good work. Each time I meet such a person, I thank them, but I also express my sadness. I tell them that I wish they had written even one letter to the programme, to the papers, to me, expressing their pride and pleasure when it could have helped me, helped balance the tide of racist letters which bolstered the excuse with which I was dismissed.

They, simple, working-class Jamaicans of the type who tried not to rock the boat while they lived in Britain, tell me that they never thought of writing, not even to me. They never dreamed that there was a racist backlash. Only in recent years, as I meet them one by one in Jamaica, does a picture emerge of a Black audience switching on each evening just to see and hear me, in contrast to the hostility that faced me on all sides as I worked. I saw only a vast, White audience.

Though Alex had undoubtedly justified hiring me because of the large Black London audience, it was a very silent and invisible audience, cowed into silence by their desperate need to live down the bad press of Notting Hill and Brixton's riots.

The West Indian population had learned that in any confrontation the White aggressors, no matter how much in the wrong, would always be presented as the innocent angels, victims of the savagery which was to be expected from Blacks only a generation removed from the cannibalism of their wild jungle lives . . . the Great White Fear. West Indians knew that their best tactic was to express no public opinion about anything whatsoever, lest the ghosts of Notting Hill and Lucky Gordon be revived and flung into their collective faces.

Nine months later I got a similar job on the *Today* nightly programme on ATV, Birmingham. It was just like the London programme, except that the racism in Birmingham was even more intense, as that was Enoch Powell's city.

No hotel would rent me a room, so each morning I took the train from London to Birmingham, did the show, then took the train back to my London flat. After several weeks, someone found me an empty room at the city's YWCA, residence of ageing spinsters and a few people living with mental health conditions. I spent my Monday to Thursday nights there and my weekends in London after Friday's show.

Birmingham and the Midlands region of Britain were a vast contrast to multicultural London. The racism appeared in the prejudices which the show's staffers tried unsuccessfully to hide, but all I cared about was doing my job and getting paid.

I came back to the studio one evening from an outside film shoot to learn that Enoch Powell had been interviewed live on the show, after agreeing to appear on the programme as long as I was neither on the show nor in the studio. When my six-month contract ended, it was not renewed.

I returned to England in 1982, ten years after I had left as the sole Black face on British television, its 'token nigger'. Ten years later, there was not a single Black host or hostess of a TV programme, whether light entertainment, current affairs or whatever, though ITN did employ a Trinidadian news reader. It took the advent of Channel 4 (under the same Jeremy Isaacs) to stir up British television enough for programmes and presenters of West Indian origin to become widespread.

In the intervening ten years there had been few programmes directed at the vast immigrant population, or attempting to portray in a positive light their cultural origins and social contributions, other than as singers and dancers, or the occasional anthropological foray into the ghettoes at times of social unrest, or to the islands on 'where they came from' stories designed to give the programme producers a holiday in the sun.

I view this as a deliberate insult to the Black population of a country which constantly tries to make you believe that it is not racist. The political stance taken by successive British governments in favour of lenient behaviour towards the renegade Ian Smith only served to bolster the impression that the British wished we could staff their buses and psychiatric hospitals, sweep the streets and empty the garbage, without actually living, giving birth and wishing to participate equally in their lily-White country.

Needless to say, I had no such strong feelings in February 1969, as I contemplated my unemployed status. There was no Race Relations Board to which I could complain, or equal-opportunity clause to support the integration of the programme. Just like my West Indian brethren I meekly accepted my fate, thankful that at least I had been allowed to raise my Black head so daringly, though briefly, on their glorious television screens.

What would it take, you might well ask at this point, for me to change from this attitude?

A kick in the ass, I would answer.

But this was not to come for a while yet, so I continued in blissful optimism.

So this had been 'the break'!

Well, since I had not let it go to my head, had not let it change my lifestyle, I could consider it not an end – as some may have wished me to – but a brand-new beginning.

Chapter Eleven

My earnings had not been so great that I had saved much money, despite my brave comments to the *Sunday Times* reporter. I genuinely hoped that, as the article said, another producer would want to employ me. But the months passed without any frantic knocking on my professional door, so I turned to straight journalism for a source of income.

Now that I had a 'name', I found it easy to persuade editors that I should be allowed to write for them, and began a good relationship with such publications as *Queen* magazine, the *Daily Mail* and the *Sunday Times*, in its 'Look' feature section, as well as with the prestigious colour magazine. 'Look' was the most popular Sunday newspaper feature section under its editor Hunter Davies, and they paid the best rates of all publications.

Hunter ran a series called 'Me and My Money' featuring interviews with rich and famous people. He sent me to interview Sammy Davis Jr for the column, as he was at Twickenham Studios filming *Salt and Pepper* with Peter Lawford. A chauffeured limousine took me to the set and later, over a very good lunch at a nearby country inn with various people fluttering around him, I conducted my interview.

I had met Sammy Davis Jr one morning ten years before in Jamaica, when a girlfriend had taken me with her to the Stony Hill Hotel where he was staying during a series of shows in Kingston. Soon after we arrived at a hotel suite full of musicians, my friend and all the other people departed and I found myself alone with Sammy Davis Jr for an entire day. I was alarmed, as I was only seventeen, very shy and with no knowledge of how to handle the situation. This was no seduction, however. I think he must have just wanted some time alone to himself, for he spent the day saying very little other than small talk with a pleasant smile.

Most of the time he spent cleaning his several cameras, and explaining how some piece of equipment worked. I think he took a few snaps of me, although I couldn't be sure that film was in the camera he clicked. He showed me some of his photographs, especially one of his wife, the Swedish actress May Britt, and we talked about his children and about Jamaica. We ate an early dinner, at which he presented me with a single peach-coloured rose. Then the limousine arrived to take us to the Carib Theatre where he was performing, and my day with Sammy Davis had ended.

This time, when I finished asking him questions for my article, I shyly asked him if he remembered meeting me. He said yes, but in the way that celebrities say yes who have met thousands of people and forgotten more than half. When lunch was over and I prepared to leave, he invited me to lunch with him the next day at the Aretusa – London's leading spot. But believe it or not, I was too shy to tell him that I had neither the bus nor taxi fare to get to the restaurant, and was too stupid to tell him to send a car for me.

Underlying my refusal was the reluctance to have my photo splashed across the tabloids as 'Sammy Davis Jr's girlfriend'. (It was a similar reluctance that made me turn down similar invitations on other occasions from film actor Rod Steiger, singer Stevie Wonder, boxer Ken Norton and film star Jim Brown, but those are other stories to be told.)

I interviewed Jacqueline Susann, the author of *Valley of the Dolls* in her suite at the Dorchester Hotel overlooking Park Lane. She was in London to promote her new book *The Love Machine*, whose cover featured a hand wearing a gold ankh ring, the Egyptian symbol of love and fertility. When I admired the ring during our very friendly conversation, she promptly dashed into her bedroom and came out with one for me, saying she had intended it as a present for a friend in Switzerland, but wanted me to have it. She also showed me her coat, a khaki trench coat lined in mink, a present from her very loving husband. Jacqueline Susann was a lovely person, full of life and bubbling over with enthusiasm. When she died a year later, I was surprised to read that both she and her husband had known for several years that she had an incurable cancer.

One of the articles I wrote for the *Sunday Times* that got quite a lot of notoriety was about the 'cap' method of birth control.

Remember, this was the Swinging Sixties, when Women's Lib was born and the contraceptive pill provided women with new methods of birth control that removed some of the psychological hang-ups about sex.

Around this time too, I became good friends with John and Liz Pringle. He was a wealthy White Jamaican who conceptualized and built the famous Round Hill Hotel, haven of the wealthy jet set whose villa owners included Noël Coward and Fred Astaire. John had been appointed Director of the Jamaica Tourist Board and had transformed Jamaican travel into a classy and successful destination for the wealthy, not least of all because of his glamorous wife Liz, a Canadian who had been the world's top model before she married John and gave up her career to be his extremely elegant hostess.

When John resigned as Tourism Director, they moved to London where John became head of the London office of Doyle Dane Bernbach, then the US leading advertising agency which also handled the Jamaica tourism account. John transformed the agency from a dull organization into Britain's number one, redecorating the offices in a bright modern style, and hiring the best talent money could buy. I still remember the memorable DDB opening party, attended by the elite of show business and business.

John's style and Liz's glamour made them fit perfectly into the upper levels of London's swinging society, while their political and Jamaican connections gave seal of nobility to their frequent entertaining sessions. Liz was by far the most beautiful and self-possessed woman I knew and the fact that John was Jamaican made invitations to their house a real pleasure.

The Pringles had bought a house in Knightsbridge from a wealthy US film producer, and Liz used her impeccable taste to decorate the four floors beautifully. Their house was true luxury; I have never been in a more elegant dwelling. I remember most of all the walls and walls of cupboards in the basement kitchen, which contained several different sets of china for different styles of eating, crystal glasses of all shapes and value, pots, pans, serving dishes, breakfast sets, dinner sets, lunch sets, in a never-ending assortment. Liz was also a very good cook and sometimes I was allowed to prepare a meal using the excellent equipment.

The walls of the house were hung with Haitian and Jamaican primitive paintings of excellent taste and value. Their record collection included Bessie Smith, Billie Holiday and other nostalgia from the days of Round Hill's jet set.

I read a lot of books by Blacks that spring, back in London. 'Black is Beautiful' was becoming a popular phrase. Black men on the streets of London started wearing Afro hairstyles and dashikis, both of which were very revolutionary actions. Huey Newton had written *Seize the Time*, encouraging and justifying Black American men carrying guns to defend themselves against the racist system. I read about the shoot-outs they defiantly engaged in, and marvelled at their urban guerrilla bravery.

Eldridge Cleaver had confessed how wrong he had been to be straightening his hair and loving White women in *Soul on Ice*, a book written from his jail cell, a location that was rapidly becoming THE place from which important Black statements were made.

Most of all, a young Black woman named Angela Davis had become America's Most Wanted Person for the part she had played in the escape attempt of three young Black prisoners. Her arrest and subsequent imprisonment were becoming a worldwide cause which was exposing the ways in which the American system used racial excuses to jail those Black men who were daring enough to lash out in any way against 'the system' for their survival.

Maybe, I thought, it was time to go home and see if things had changed enough for me to make a permanent return. I offered to write an article on my visit for the *Sunday Times Magazine*, and on the strength of this the Jamaica Tourist Board said they would give me a week's free accommodation on the North Coast.

My flatmate at the time, Martin, was a crazily nice young man whose girlfriend had worked with me as a researcher on the *Today* show, and was himself a researcher with another TV station. He said he felt like seeing Jamaica, which I talked so much about, so I said by all means come along, I'd love the company. Later, as I have already said, I learned that the rumour when we both arrived in Jamaica was that he was my fiancé, even though he did not share my north coast holiday or stay in the same house in Kingston.

The article on my trip became a full-colour feature in the *Sunday Times* on my return, but Jamaica was aghast at its contents. I had spoken about how pot-holed the roads were, and had dared to criticize the monopoly by people from Development Minister Edward Seaga's constituency of cultural awards in the Independence Festival.

The general response to my article was nothing short of a national heart attack. The fact that I had ended by saying how glad I was to be returning to England was my final condemnation. But what had I said that wasn't the truth? That in 1970 the Tourist Board was still promoting a Jamaica of slaves and White gods, a false unreal world of asparagus and snails, when

Americans wanted to experience the real Jamaica of reggae and village feasts, not 'Yellow Bird' and 'Jamaica Farewell'. Wasn't that the truth?

Backward, behind the times with their heads like ostriches in the white sand, Jamaica's tourist board mentality was not ready for me, nor I for it. Jamaica was still in exactly the same place in which I had left it six years before. The growing Black Consciousness movement had definitely not reached Jamaica, and it seemed that any sign of it would be bitterly fought against by the White-minded executives of the Tourist Board.

I was not even then aware that the repressive political policies of the ruling regime had banned all Black Conscious literature from Jamaica's shores as subversive, even Alex Haley's biography of Malcolm X!

All I knew was that, coming from the harshness of Birmingham and British racism, which gave no love whatsoever to Black people, it rankled me to see for the first time the true reality of our persistent slave mentality which still gave fawning service to White people and pandered to every decadent whim with an air of subservient gratitude, to thank Whites for doing themselves the favour of visiting Jamaica. Here indeed was the beautiful Jamaica I had boasted about, the Jamaica where we were truly nice to White people, the Jamaica that had no idea just how grim and painful life was for Jamaicans at the hands of the very race to whom we bowed and scraped with such eagerness at the urging of our tourism masters.

But the power of such backward people seemed entrenched, everlasting, impossible to be changed. Certainly three weeks did not give me much time to look beneath the surface of Jamaica, but my article was accurate and truthful and written with serious sorrow. No, Jamaica was not ready for me. I would make a permanent home in England and, like Angela Davis, fight to change British racism as best I could.

Such was my noble, if naïve, ideal.

What made the new Black men I was reading about so attractive was that they appeared like a totally new breed: newborn; proud; defiant; bold; strong; Black. I was comparing them with the beaten and humble older Blacks on London streets, the younger hustlers with their White women, the youths who couldn't figure out where they were in the system: English or West Indian. I was admiring these new Blacks with their heads thrown back, looking you straight in the eye and speaking about something other than sex, telling me I was beautiful just because I was Black. This was something new; something disturbing in a nice way.

They gave me a tingling feeling, this new breed of African warriors, and as a woman of their race I was curious about them.

Men!

Such a problem.

I still only had White boyfriends. My boyfriend while I was working in Birmingham had been a nice, good-looking, modest man – an architect – who really loved me and wrote the most beautiful love letters from London. His mother, a happy and down-to-earth person, had made it a point to meet me and to introduce me to HER mother, taking the train to Birmingham with me one morning and taking me by taxi to meet her Mam.

They were all really nice people, happy that I was their son's woman. She knitted me a lovely pair of warm white socks when I told her about my chilblains, which was a gift I truly appreciated. But much as I liked him, he just wasn't my ideal man. In the back of my mind I was always evaluating a man by whether I could take him back to Jamaica, whether he would fit. None did, no matter how long it took me to evaluate them.

Could I be Mrs Famous Athlete? Or Lady That?

Lord, no. I would be laughed to scorn.

Mrs Celebrity's wife?

Definitely not.

I certainly intended to become a celebrity in my own right, not hang on the name and status of some famous person. I wanted no notoriety, just a quiet guy who would fit in equally in the place I wanted to occupy in Jamaica: not too high, not too low. A Jamaican? I couldn't see a suitable one yet, one at least of my own status and social background. So men were definitely not my immediate priority.

It was 1970. I was out of work, though a mini-celebrity, recognized on the street, though I wanted anonymity. I also now possessed a turned-on conscience. I realized I had a 'responsibility' and moreover, perhaps, an 'opportunity' to do something, to try and change the racial opinion people had of us, and also to help my own Black people in some way to raise themselves up. I know this sounds high-minded, but it was not so conceived. It's just that I realized that I was part of a lame team, and could help. I was lame both psychologically and racially, but especially economically.

No money. No work.

A disinterested agent couldn't be bothered to try very hard to find new work for me. That was cool. I couldn't see any possibilities either. I was content to exist by falling back on the Brook Street Bureau. I got a temporary job with an advertising agency. I didn't mind the secretarial work. It was honest, steady money. Being a temporary employee, I wasn't obliged to form friendships with the people I met, nor they with me. I was content to inhabit my protective, routine-encased world, well ordered for self-sufficiency. I knew where the buses and tubes were, and the language of eating alone. I was okay.

I started trying to find out what was going on in the Black West Indian community. Notting Hill, where I was still living, was the one area of London where Blacks and Whites were truly at ease with each other.

Time had healed many scars and also exposed the weaknesses and strengths of each side, so a peace had been declared. In this operated both the old elements of Black hustling, and also the nucleus of a small but militant local Black Power movement led by Blacks educated into Marxist-Leninist socialist consciousness.

Headquartered in a shop at the Black end of Portobello Road, where old clothes were sold, was a bookshop where members of a socialist co-operative sold books, booklets and pamphlets about the US Black civil rights struggle and Marxism, as well as fierce writings on the state of British racism. Their living hero was Trinidadian author C. L. R. James who, from his Brixton home, led the Black British intellectual struggle against racism.

Knowing from reading about the war being waged by the US

intelligence powers against this struggle, that undoubtedly this local operation was closely watched by the British equivalent of the FBI, it was not without some fear that I walked slowly up the Portobello Road one Saturday, peered nervously inside the shop, and then entered, prepared to join 'the revolution'.

The group's leaders were present, as well as some supporters and fans. I introduced myself and hesitatingly started a conversation, but it was not long before I realized that they knew who I was and were firmly rejecting me. With open scorn and contempt, they laughed at my efforts at 'getting-to-know-you'. One of them, in a very, very British accent, said words to the effect that 'Whites are our enemies. We know you have been associating with them and in many ways are almost like them, so we don't want you to try and come over to our side now.' I am not too sure they didn't hurl a taunt or two at my departing back.

So much for Black Power, English West Indian style. After that experience, I kept my distance. Trying to get to my Black roots was not going to be easy.

Ten years later in 1982 I returned to that same Portobello Road headquarters to invite one of these same people to be interviewed for my Channel 4 documentary film *Race, Rhetoric, Rastafari*, only to find that their attitude had not changed. Still laughing, they refused to participate, rejecting Rastafari as a ridiculous philosophy of misguided fools, and maintaining that Marxist-Leninist Socialism was the only true pathway for Blacks.

But by then Socialism had been discredited in its Jamaican experiment, the Manley government losing the election because of local and international fears of its close ties with Communist

Cuba. The Berlin Wall was soon to fall, and shortly thereafter Russia abandoned Socialism, ending its influence and implementation in the world. It is therefore highly amusing for me today to see that the London Marxist group's leader has now grown his dreadlocks, moved to Jamaica and is working to build a new image as a pseudo Rastafari intellectual at the University of the West Indies! Those who know his true origins can only laugh.

Time longer than rope. (Jamaican saying.)

Chapter Twelve

I had been smoking pot for quite some time. First, I had smoked it as part of the Flower Power trip, when no musical or social experience was complete without first getting high and experiencing life on the other plane of existence that such an action revealed. You could not only have the fun of being alive and going about normal activities, but you also had the pleasure of having your brain operate on a deeper sensory level. Life was filtered to let in only good vibrations, whether it was simply the beauty of a sunny day, or the hidden meaning in a Beatles song. Mostly, pot enhanced the pleasure of being with friends, similar 'heads'.

But, as everyone who smokes knows, the minute you leave off fun activities and turn your mind to serious, deeper thoughts, the magnifying effect of the smoke produces equally magnified seriousness. A mature smoker also realizes the telepathic effect that smoking creates between smokers.

I had visits from two girlfriends that spring. Vonetta came over from filming in Rome, and Rhea, my Jewish American girlfriend, arrived at the same time from New York. I was greatly boosted by the strong vibrations which we all gave off because of each other's company.

We three lunched together in a bright, white, airy Italian restaurant, laughing and drinking dry white wine and enjoying the admiration of other diners envying our happiness. We were like a powerful team, we three so different women. Rhea, a zany and wonderful blonde woman, worrying that turning forty was going to mean the loss of her beauty and femininity; Vonetta, a glamorous, together Black woman, seemingly possessing everything she wanted, especially the unceasing admiration of every man in sight; and me, their pleasantly eccentric Jamaican friend and London base. But after their departure, depression returned.

To add to my own troubles, my friends the Pringles were breaking up. It was farewell to a part of my life. They had by now moved to an apartment overlooking Hyde Park which was even more beautiful than the first. Even though it only occupied one floor, it was larger than the Knightsbridge house. Liz had used her exquisite taste and John's money converting it into such a miracle that, when they put it up for sale, Ava Gardner the movie star bought it and lived there until she died.

What happened between John and Liz is their private affair, but I found myself in the unfortunate position of friend in the middle, not knowing how to help and possibly making the situation worse by thinking that I could remain a friend to both as they split. Each wanted me to see their side of the situation, while I only wanted them to remain the secure, beautiful family they had always been.

I remember, though, a night during that tense period when I had gone to visit Liz and tried to offer a diversion by asking her to show me her jewellery, which I had always admired in pieces. She led me to the large dressing room beside the bedroom, opened a door of the wall-to-wall cupboards and pulled out several slim drawers. Piece by piece she showed me her collection of rings, necklaces, earrings and other decorations: here were the diamonds, rubies, emeralds, topazes, pearls, sapphires, small pieces, large pieces, long chains of stones, small clusters of sparkling coloured lights. I had never seen such beauty or so much wealth before in one place.

I was thinking ruefully of my two or three self-bought silver ornaments, wondering how some women could be so lucky, when she said: 'Barbara, it all means nothing – the love of a man is worth much more. I'd swap all of this for that.'

It made me realize that wealth could not be measured by money, and for the first time I realized the value of that elusive commodity – LOVE.

I am truly glad to report that in time John and Liz came together again, and even re-married, though by then I was no longer part of their lives. They finally accepted that no matter what had happened they had the perfect marriage I and all their friends thought they had, and wished we could have also.

I ventured into areas which had just been names to me before, to Streatham, Kilburn, Islington, in search of Black causes I could help. All I found were young Black children cowering like rats in crowded, damp basement 'clubs' where they gathered in safety from the streets above, on which the police had too often roughed them up for 'loitering' or 'suss' (suspicious person).

The battering they had received from all corners of society, parents afraid of the White man's system, teachers who gave their education the lowest priority, jobless futures, hostile police, was written all over their faces, few of which bore any trace of the beauty that Blackness was supposed to be.

I couldn't help them.

I had no power.

I was no one.

They needed a greater help, they needed a society that would see them as equal human beings and give them the chance to live equally, not as rats in a hole.

How could I help? I couldn't even afford the bus fare. It was a massive problem that would have to be dealt with by the ever-increasing numbers of social welfare officers, teachers and politicians.

There was one bright lily trying to grow up in the pigsty, a theatre club for Black cultural expression called Keskidee, run by a fatherlike West Indian, Oscar. By the skin of his teeth Oscar was putting on plays, rehearsing poetry and songs, and generally providing a place where the continuous activity and home-like atmosphere was encouraging neighbourhood problem kids to identify with their culture.

It was housed in a barn-like church hall, with no heating, but it eventually grew into a place of quiet cultural pleasure, painted walls, canteen, library and central heating. Oscar's hard work deserved such success. In 1971 playwrights like Wole Soyinka, Pat

Maddy and even the slightly crazy Alfred Fagon were among the Black artists who frequented Keskidee and gave of their cultural best to its growth.

Another artist contributing to Keskidee's growth was Anton Phillips, my Jamaican 'brother' who had now graduated from drama school and started his career as a good, serious Black actor. When Ed Bullins, an avant-garde Black American playwright and director, produced a Black version of *Othello*, Anton played Iago as a hip, jive-talking nigger dude who laid a lot of Black rap on Uncle Tom Othello to try and persuade him not to be so dumb as to kill himself over that White broad. It was good theatre and he was good in it.

Still the question remained: why was happiness so elusive if one was Black? I couldn't answer that question. I couldn't understand the logic that said that, like a curse, the Black person was forever condemned to live in suffering. The truths that I was now able to see showed that we did not deserve suffering as a reward for the way in which we had endured meekly the transgressions inflicted upon us by the White race. They had taken us as slaves, brutalized us, stolen our wealth from the earth and from the flesh. They had turned our countries into servants for their cities and now, when we came among them seeking the 'freedom' they said they had given us, they rewarded us, not with remorseful equality, but rather contempt and hatred.

It was this constant contempt that prevented us from seeing our worth as a race and as individuals. Under such a burden, even the brightest sparks would fizzle. I felt my spark fizzling.

*

War photographer Don McCullin selected me as his choice to answer the question 'What Is Beauty?', to which the *Sunday Times Magazine* devoted an entire issue. I posed for him in the living room of the house in which I was helping Patrick Lichfield operate a crazy personal mail-delivery service – complete with stamps featuring his aristocratic crest – during a London Post Office strike. I couldn't believe the beautiful things Don said to me as he photographed me, surprised at such gentleness and beauty in a man who had made an international name photographing war and death.

The magazine captioned my photo: 'The understated elegance of Barbara Blake . . .' I was the only Black (again!) among such company as Jean Shrimpton, Twiggy, Rudolf Nureyev, Mick Jagger and other better- and lesser-known luminaries. But was mine really beauty? I kept asking myself.

A women's glossy magazine photographed and interviewed me smiling widely in its series 'Women who have happily matched a fashion style to their lives and personalities'.

I wrote in *Queen*: 'Whatever Happened to Superman?', a frivolous, supposedly humorous piece done for the money in *Queen* style, which described many types of the men one could expect to meet in the most sought-after circles, but when I carefully scrutinized the article, I realized that what I was saying was that there really were no men around.

Boys, by the multitude, yes.

Sexually sick people. Yes, yes.

Users, often.

But lovers, bold, masculine, strong men . . . no.

Still waiting for Superman, I decided it was time to move from the Chepstow Road groove. Perhaps life would change with a new address. I saw an ad in an underground paper offering to swap a loft for a two-bedroom and called the number. Soon, a hippie couple came to see my flat, and in turn I went to see theirs.

The address was great – a narrow street opposite the main entrance of Selfridges on Oxford Street in the heart of London. I had to walk up four high flights of stairs in an old building, to find the loft at the top. It was a very large room, in a corner of which the couple had erected a sleeping platform. There was a sloping roof which was partly covered with a glass skylight, by now so old that it let in little light. There was a window on one wall.

But what transfixed me like a magnet was one wall on which they had painted a mystical, stoned, Flower Power painting of a woman. I agreed to swap flats. I moved in and instantly regretted it. Frightened and alone in the cold dark room, surrounded by boxes of belongings and piles of filthy rubbish left behind by the hippies, I wondered whether I had done the right thing.

The bath was an old metal urn with a bench seat in it, over which hung the most ancient gas water heater and spigot which looked as if it was about to explode. In the bath itself was a coating of body fat which took me two weeks of filling up with hot water, bleach and disinfectant on a daily basis to get clean enough to overcome my total revulsion and cleanse my body in it.

As if that was not enough, among the piles of rubbish were literally hundreds of empty coffee bottles. God knows what they had intended to use them for, but I was left with the task of persuading the garbage men to make several laborious flights early one morning to clear away the filth. At that point, I laid down new wall-to-wall brown carpet, and for the first time in about two weeks, my near hysteria subsided.

I had a job as a secretary, relieving a girlfriend of mine who worked for two guys who made TV commercials. Their office was in fashionable Curzon Street off Park Lane. The back entrance opened out into Shepherd Market, a quaint, high-class area of cobbled stone streets and old houses which housed the city's most expensive call girls. I found out this when I asked why it was that each time I went out to buy lunch or cigarettes, a lot of middle-aged men in three-piece suits sniffed around me or stared in my face in open question. Crazy people.

It was the winter of the Chi-Lites hit 'Have You Seen Her' and it was fitting for my mood that the number one song was by a Black group. My move to the loft was a first step in the cutting off of a lot of old ways, a lot of old friends, a period of introspection made necessary by the growing process that was going on in me.

As I cleared floor space and tried to make some order each night as I returned from work, the flat began to be comfortable. I put a spare mattress on the floor and covered it with an Indian spread. There were huge brown cushions too, and multi-coloured Habitat cube box couches, dried flowers in my precious Victorian water jug, a yellow-framed mirror on one wall, and on another wall the ornate gilt mirror with a cherub flying on top and a shelf with candle holders beneath which John and Liz had given me.

I draped my rainbow-coloured sari on the overhead beam, and hung my careful pencil drawing of chrysanthemums on the wall by the fireplace. I had high hopes to make the place really comfortable, rebuild the sleeping platform with even pieces of good wood instead of odds and ends, to put in a real kitchen and shelf, and to install a shower. But I knew that it would take much more money than I had to make these changes. Moreover, I felt I should now be in the position to buy a flat for myself, not just trying to repair something that should have been condemned long ago.

As the loft began to be comfortable, I began to think of my future in England.

Where had I gone wrong?

Why had I not entered the financial big time, when all the notoriety came by? I did not realize that it would have taken a different person, with a good support team, to claw their way from the Black side into the closed White circle.

So I asked myself if I was a failure.

The regular pot-smoking I was doing didn't help either. What was happening to me, as happens to everyone when they start smoking, was that I was asking myself questions that I could not answer, questions about myself, about who I was, what I was doing, and how well I was playing the game of life. The answers that were coming back were not nice ones.

The answers said that to live in this White world, trying to be like White people and to be liked by them, was a false effort, a hypocrisy, and nothing to be aspired to. The answers said that I deserved to be scorned and disliked by both White AND Black people. The answers said that it was time to stop trying to be like White people.

They hadn't shown me they were nice people to be like.

(Later in my life, I learned that this same rule could and should be applied in my own society towards those whose unlovable behaviour I had felt obliged to respect, though not totally imitate, and that to step away from 'society' was often a most rewarding act.)

But how to step away, I did not know. My only awareness of an alternative lifestyle was the musical images that were being created of Black love by such artists as Roberta Flack, Curtis Mayfield, Isaac Hayes, Marvin Gaye. Those of us with no Black blueprints on how to shed the old masks and put on the new ones could only grope blindly towards the light at the end of this glorious musical tunnel, and thus I spent a lot of time listening to music and contemplating my options.

Showing a White American girlfriend a photo of me, I asked with my usual laugh if she didn't think I looked good. In reply she said: 'Barbara, why don't you let your hair go natural?'

I realized that she was not only serious, but also my friend.

It was a question I could not answer, because I realized suddenly that straightened hair was truly designed to make a Black woman feel as nearly White as she could be.

Why had I resisted so long? If only I had known about the beautiful, soft, glossy black curls that would later adorn my head, growing more beautiful each day as my natural hair grew out. If only I had known how nice it would be to touch, how pleasant to groom, how easy to comb and style. If only I had known how happy it would make me.

I guess it must be like baptism, or believing in Life Everlasting. Until you do it, you think it is something far too difficult for you to ever accomplish, something that will make you look ridiculous.

I was locked into the great hair fear, brainwashed into feeling shame at exposing the real black fuzz, the shame of the 'picka-peppa grains' showing instead of shiny straight stiff lines of pretend White hair, how rough it would feel, how 'ugly' it would make me look.

Men would probably stop liking me.

No.

I couldn't.

Or could I?

On 1 January, New Year's Day, I took the bus to St Clair's new salon at Marble Arch to go through my twice-yearly ritual of straightening.

Lorna loved to have my infrequent visits, not only because I had remained her friend from the less luxurious beginnings, but because she was proud to have a real Black 'celebrity' in her salon. Most of all, she liked to show off her skills on my sleek and long hair. She and George were really nice people.

On 17 January 1972, I went back to Lorna.

'Cut it all off,' I told her.

She almost fainted.

'You're not SERIOUS!'

But I was.

I had made up my mind. I had made a decision to stop trying to be White. Inside me, I was beginning to understand what being Black meant. Outside, the message I sent was a contradiction of my inner feelings. For better or worse, the time had come to take the hair plunge. It was important.

I sat in silence as George and Lorna took turns cutting off my hair. It hurt them to do it. As it grew shorter and shorter, I silently wondered how it would eventually look. Would it end up shabby and dull, or would I be fortunate enough to have the thick bush of Angela Davis?

My mind flashed to the beautiful mane of Marsha Hunt, the fabulous Black girl who starred in the sensational musical *Hair*, and I realized the appropriateness of the title of that important and liberating theatrical event, for hair was indeed the central emblem of the political and social battles of the world. First the hippies had defied society by growing their hair long and free, now the Black man and woman were using their natural hairstyle to demonstrate their attitude of Black Power to the startled world.

Hair had become a symbol of the militant Black stance, an emblem that demonstrated just who was prepared to stand behind the new positive Black attitudes that were being articulated. Natural black hair was an open statement that said: here I am, Black, naked, no pretension, no desire to ape Whitey. Bearing our natural hairstyles was as defiant a statement as if we had taken up spears or had guns at the ready.

Yes, I wanted to be counted among the new breed of Black warriors, male and female, for I too was at war. At war with the White English society that had no room for me.

When Lorna finished, it didn't look too bad. After all, there was still a lot of straightening in it. I was content. I felt cleansed, different, new.

Lorna almost wept.

Panic set in a week later, when I washed it for the first time. It was like the shock I experienced when I washed my hair after its very first straightening. As I surveyed the total chaos on top of my head, it was easy to regret having taken such a drastic action. I had hoped it would fall into shiny curls, but instead as it dried it became duller and frizzier and uglier.

You know, it's hard to re-tell these experiences. At this time of writing, seven years later, my hair is a beauty asset envied by Black and White women. In the years when I still combed it out, it was soft, silky, long, shiny and had enough 'straight' in it to make it lie down in neat lines, when I wished. I used to sweep it up into one topknot and when I combed that out and shook my head, it was like a rippled halo. I started becoming vain about my 'pretty hair', but when I returned to Jamaica and started living as a Rasta, I covered up every strand to overcome the vanity before I eventually started growing my locks when my son was born in 1985.

Today my locks are below my knees and I have had the pleasure of growing it out for twenty-four years, as I write, bringing another dimension of beauty to my hair and hairstyle. So, it's hard now to recall the panic of those first weeks and months of growing-out hair. The self-hate, the feeling of ugliness, the feeling of not knowing what the future held for my looks, what style would be created, what texture, what look. It was a mystery of faith, like contemplating death and the life after.

It was in this state of depression that I greeted my former flatmate Beverley Anderson, who phoned to say she was in London. I invited her over for lunch. It had been six years since we last spoke and I was surprised that she was back in London.

I wished I could have hidden my ugliness, as I contemplated her sleek, henna-coloured, straightened hair, no longer covered in her trademark Sophia Loren wig of London days, but now slicked back into a bun at the nape of her neck. She looked at my 'Afro' and laughed. Afros were definitely 'out' in Jamaica, she told me. Nina Simone performed in Jamaica with an Afro and everyone laughed at her hairstyle.

But Beverley wanted to do more than talk about hair. When she told me her news, I could understand why she was in London. She was shopping for her forthcoming marriage to, guess who!

Michael Manley!

Well, fancy that!

How interesting life could be!

Michael, who one fully expected would – if marrying again at all – be choosing some White Jamaican society beauty, choosing instead a Black woman, my friend Beverley of Turnpike Lane and our crazy South Kensington flat. Memories of chilblains, the boys from the Economist Intelligence Unit, sausages and mash meals, and a suitcase of clothes under the bed, made me smile.

Michael Manley was the most famous man in Jamaica, even though he was only Leader of the Opposition, not the Prime Minister he would soon become, but he was handsome and had quite a reputation as a ladies' man. I had met him once, when John Pringle asked me as a favour to organize a press conference for him on his way back from a trip to Africa, carrying a carved rod he later claimed to have been given to him by Ethiopian Emperor Haile Selassie, and which became a famous prop for his election campaign.

I completed John's favour, inviting some Fleet Street journalists with an interest in Caribbean politics, then rushing out afterwards to meet my boyfriend for a late lunch. But the favour also included me taking Michael for drinks that night at the Playboy Club, newly opened in London, for entry to which one needed a membership card which I had earned from modelling some Jamaican clothes there a few weeks earlier. The Playboy Club wasn't exactly my type of nightlife, but John thought it was perfect for Michael, so I escorted him there, spent a couple of hours with him ogling the scantily dressed Bunnies, and then dropped him off at his hotel before heading home. Jamaican politicians were definitely not my type!

But I wished Beverley happiness. With no emotional feelings whatsoever for Michael Manley, I had no envy for her good fortune. The news of her visit later appeared in a British newspaper column, which created quite a scandal not just because Beverley was Black and marrying a Prime Minister, but because no announcement of the controversial engagement had yet been made in Jamaica.

(I later learned that when the scandal broke in Jamaica, I was accused of having placed the newspaper story. Not so. The most likely culprit was Manley's daughter Rachel, whose recent marriage to a rich, distant relation of the royal family had placed her under the scrutiny and in the company of such society journalists, who had labelled her 'a dusky beauty' to inform everyone that she had Black blood despite her White skin. I stayed far from these prejudiced circles.)

I thought about the new life Beverley was going to be living, so different from mine, but no less interesting, I was sure. I was embarking on a totally different journey. My friendship with

Vonetta the movie star had already given me a chance to observe a girlfriend live out what could have been my own reality and see how closely that reality compared with the trip I would have taken down that road.

My choice was the start of a journey of Black discovery.

I would not be content until I reached its end.

Its beginning had been quite painful.

Surely things would improve.

Alone in my flat, I endured agonies of self-castigation. My friends Anton and Sonia must have grown tired of my lengthy, crazy, panic-filled, late-night phone calls, full of my doubts and fears.

My hair didn't add to my self-esteem.

As the natural parts grew out, the battered, straightened ends had to be cut off. The natural parts that were growing out were also beaten and battered, and refused to be anything but dull, dull and stiff, stiff. They had to be cut, cut, cut until new growth beneath grew out.

My head looked like a reddish straw doormat. Getting used to the crinkly texture of my hair was also new. It felt strange, looked strange after these years of feeling 'straight'.

Had I really been being White?

Had I really been trying to be White?

With hindsight, I can realize that I WAS in fact being a Black girl all the time. Black, as far as the pattern that had been shown to me. I was absolutely no different from the hundreds and thousands of similar Black girls and women who had been brought up to believe that to imitate Whites was normal behaviour for a Black person.

Within this amazing confinement, I actually functioned in my limited way as a Black person, or at least like a Jamaican, reacting to things that were strange to the decent Black feelings I had been brought up with, reacting like a stranger in a White world. But, like all Blacks at our stage of development, I contained the deeply taught philosophy that a Black person's position was automatically and perpetually second to the White, and apparently every other race also.

This philosophy had stunted my growth and created a set of responses which were false in appearance as well as intention, even though I had an adventurous and rebellious spirit. All that was happening was that I was now letting go of the falseness. I had to do a lot of analysing to see just where the falseness was.

It was like shedding a skin, a re-birth from a womb of Blackness.

It was terrible, but it was beautiful.

It was amazing what a difference my hairstyle made.

It became nice to go out into the street and be hailed by a brother, 'Hi, sister.'

Or just a look, and a nodded hello.

It became nice.

Like having emerged from baptism, fresh and clean.

On an impulse, I went to see Desmond Wilcox, producer of *Man Alive*, the leading weekly BBC current affairs documentary programme that had a reputation for fearlessness in reporting, and a team considered the best in the industry. I asked him for a job as a researcher.

To my surprise, he agreed. I found myself once again in television.

I had a job! Income and respectability!

This time, it was my job to find the story and hand it prepared to the reporter. *Man Alive* had a big reputation. As my first assignment, I was told to bring in a story on old age pensioners.

Oops, said my fellow workers. This is a test for you. They considered such a topic a hard one to find anything interesting or new to make a story about. But somehow, I didn't mind. Content to be left alone, I set about finding some old age pensioners who might make a representative story, and gathering all the facts about how they lived and what legislation was pending which might make their much-complained-about lives better.

It proved to be quite an educative experience for me. In the course of the story, I found myself in the most miserable places I had ever had the misfortune to experience. No Kingston ghetto room can compare with the misery and poverty in which some dying old people live in England. People lived in one or two smelly rooms of cold and damp, with only a bird or a cat as company, existing on six pounds a week with scraps of food for sustenance.

Most had been abandoned by their offspring, in a society where the extended family unit of parents, children and grandparents had long ago been replaced by the efficiency and economy of the welfare state. The smell of decay, the sights of rags of clothes, bad plumbing, bodies unwashed for days and weeks, was pitiful.

I selected three subjects: an aged, gay entertainer living in Notting Hill; a 'distressed gentlewoman' from the suburbs; and, loveliest of all, an old couple from the industrial town of Chorley in Lancashire. They were the nicest people I ever met in England, two humble folk who had grown up, loved and lived in the same cobbled street of this mill town all their lives, and who thought I was a breeze of sunshine blown into their simple lives. Taking them to lunch at the town hotel was the greatest deed anyone had ever done them. No, it wasn't because I was from the TV, or that they were trying to show they weren't prejudiced. They were just two nice, decent people, able to give love freely without hang-ups, because they had never known any other way. They reminded me of the Welsh couple we had stayed with at a pub at Cefn Coch, Wales, when I worked with ATV.

The story was filmed. I arranged for us to have Barbara Castle, the most popular British woman MP, as chief among the studio guests for the post-film discussion, and the programme was considered quite a success. I know for certain that my astonished Jamaican eyes had seen, and therefore been able to show in the programme, the real truth of the pitiful way the old lived in England, which is why the programme had been so interesting. But it had also shown me something.

I lay back on the large brown cushions by the fire in my flat and contemplated my future. The dark shadows reflecting on the roof seemed like the darkening skies of old age. Would that be me, aged sixty, still living in this decaying flat, an eccentric Black lady at the top of the stairs, with young people brought to see me and hear my story of life?

No, I prayed.

Deliver me from that.

I didn't deserve it.

Chapter Thirteen

Easter brought a calm. I find it is always a time of refreshing renewal. All the best things in my life have happened at Easter. My hair didn't look too bad now. I had finally cut off the layer of old straightened ends, had endured weeks of cutting off red, brittle ends of new natty hair growing out from abused roots. Now finally I had set it on pencil-thin rollers with lots of conditioner. It had turned out rather cute, shiny and wavy, looking like today's Jheri curls.

Feeling good, I threw an Easter party for my friends who had children, and they made noisy fun in the flat. Rhea was in town, which was always nice, staying at the prettiest hotel, the Portobello in the fashionable part of Notting Hill. But it was another girlfriend, Tessa Topolski, daughter of the famous painter, who brought my real Easter present, a beautiful Black man. 'Barbara, I've got someone special I want you to meet. I'm bringing him to the party,' she said.

And he was special.

A Jamaican, surprisingly, handsome, full of life, laughter and style, a law student in his final year, so close to my own upbringing and background, that we both marvelled that we had not met before. If I had never before understood the meaning of 'love at first sight', I did now. I tried hard to suppress any evidence of the huge emotion I felt at his presence, though he made no effort to hide his own huge pleasure at meeting me. I couldn't have been happier. My prayers had been answered.

The months that followed were some of the sweetest of my life in England. His sweetness included a re-introduction to my own country Jamaica, an introduction to its reggae music and an update on what was happening politically, especially the full weight of Michael Manley's recent election as Prime Minister and the wonderful promises his government was making. He told me that Manley had visited the prisons and deplored the conditions, he had 'freed up ganja', and that he had come to power on the Rastafari slogan 'Peace and Love', carrying a 'rod of correction' given him by Emperor Haile Selassie during a visit to Africa.

I was surprised that Michael Manley had become a revolutionary Prime Minister! How unbelievable!

His campaign bandwagon had toured Jamaica using Rastafari slogans!

Could that really be so?

Rastafari, those ragged men with locksed hair that the Tourist Board shunned?

Yes, Rastafari was everything in Jamaica now, he explained.

Everyone seemed to be wearing red, gold and green and locksing their hair, even among the upper classes.

I was surprised. I remembered the fire-and-brimstone men

whom my father had warned me to respect, rather than scorn or run from, as was the accustomed social reaction. I remembered the Henry affair in 1961 when a group of Black Power Americans, led by the son of a Rasta elder Claudius Henry, led an attempt to take over the country; I remembered the rumble of trucks, lorries and vehicles full of British, Jamaican and West Indian soldiers and police passing our house on the way to wipe out the rebels holed up in the St Andrew hills.

I remembered the record '007 Shanty Town' about urban ghetto rebels, which my English secretary had played for me to translate the words, but which I couldn't understand.

Yet I could not conceive how those who had up till recently been so scorned, had finally been recognized as a power for good. I learned that the Rastafari love of the Bible and of God had become part of the Jamaican Revolution, and suddenly I yearned to read my Bible just like a book, from start to finish, and evaluate it like any other to see if it was all it was alleged to be.

A vision of a new Jamaica began to come into focus. It was a natural outgrowth of my growing Black Consciousness. Into the variety of life-possibilities I was contemplating, I began to contemplate the possibility of returning home to live in Jamaica.

I was also understanding how nice and different it was to be with a Black Jamaican man. Our backgrounds were so alike that we had the same intellectual and social references. On top of that, we also understood totally the Black language that was being communicated to our emotions and growth by American music, films like *Shaft* and superstars like Jim Brown. In London our social circles were similar and overlapped.

So, we enjoyed each other. I dared to hope that such happiness would be lasting.

My two friends, film-makers Ismail Merchant and James Ivory, who were just beginning a career which is now world-famous, were then known best for their classic black-and-white film *Shakespeare Wallah*, the story of a family of English Shakespearian actors living and performing in post-Empire India. Ismail, a wealthy and upper-class Indian, loved to include me in his outings to lavish dinners at the best Indian restaurants in London whenever he and James, an American, were in town.

Ismail and James told me over another lavish dinner that they had just made their first colour feature film (their third together) called *Savages*, an avant-garde, beautiful film which they were going to premiere at the Cannes Film Festival. *Playboy* magazine had done a colour spread on the film and its more eccentric characters.

I brought story of the film to the *Man Alive* weekly programme meeting with the suggestion that the show film a story on the Cannes Festival, using *Savages* as a focus. It was a wild idea, but Desmond Wilcox, *Man Alive*'s brilliant producer/director, liked it and arranged with Time Life to do a rare co-production of the programme to be shown in the USA also.

I set about creating a representative story on the Cannes Film Festival, by going into Wardour Street, the centre of British film-making in the heart of London's Soho, and speaking to as many people at top and middle levels of the industry. The director Wilcox selected agreed that we needed a top film mogul and a lesser one as the central themes of our documentary's story.

Many people did not want to be in our film, as they had heard of the journalistic scalpel with which our programme dissected stories, sometimes revealing what would have been better hidden, so they didn't want our close scrutiny. Others didn't mind. I also thought we should try to include someone from the underground film movement, a thriving sub-culture of the hippie movement.

I assumed that our film would include *Savages*, since it had been the start of the programme's idea. But the director disagreed. To my horror, he decided to replace it with two English film-makers who had a shampoo-commercial-type film called *The Miner's Daughter*. I believe the film-makers epitomized the director's personal fantasies of his future career as a film-maker.

Time has also shown that perhaps the director's decision was based on a private arrangement outside of his job. As he was the director and I the mere researcher, I had no power to change his mind, but you can imagine how I seethed at his decision, especially in the light of how things turned out.

To depict the top end of the film industry, I found the London representative of the US company, American International Pictures, then known only for its B-grade movies, but just on the threshold of its great Blacksploitation bonanza, from which it made millions. Its top mogul was Samuel Z. Arkoff.

The Cannes Film Festival and the filming of it became another of those significant experiences of my life, on many levels.

Cannes itself was a pretty little town, very French and boasting the best of everything money could buy. I had been to France twice before, once with my girlfriend 'Sperry' to pick up a French car she had bought and drive it via Calais and boat back to

England. Then on another occasion I had travelled by overnight, cross-Channel train with a Black American girlfriend to spend a few days in Paris in the company of Black American mime Hayward Coleman, who was then a student of the great Marcel Marceau.

I had practised my French on those occasions, so Cannes was merely another French city to me, albeit a very different one. The fact that Cannes sat on a beach made it unusual. The fact that that beach was covered with rich American film people and stars, with the accompaniment of hundreds of luxury yachts moored along it, made it worth stopping to look at.

Even at its humblest restaurants, the food was excellent, with the locals presenting their best at film festival time. There were wonderful goods of all kinds to be seen in the shop windows on the narrow streets off the beachfront. I bought myself two pairs of velvet jeans, one navy blue and the other bottle green because I couldn't choose one from the rich assembly of colours these stylishly cut pants came in.

Our film crew stayed in Mougins, a district in the hills overlooking Cannes near the area where flowers are grown for French perfume. Our hotel was a series of small cottages and I remember well the smell of jasmine which scented every step of the path to my cottage at the end of the trail.

Inside it each evening I would dab on the jasmine-scented Diorissimo perfume after my bath, and get dressed listening to a tape of Marvin Gaye's *What's Going On* album, words and music that rallied us Blacks to create a new and better world for our people. It was an album that my sweet man and I listened to a lot, and now that I was far away, playing the music kept me tied to him from the distance that separated us.

Each morning my job was to go down into Cannes before the crew to make arrangements and see that our filming plans were in tune for the day, and set up our locations and interviews. I liked Cannes because there were hardly any of the looks of racist animosity that one encountered minutely in London. My French was sufficient to help me out when there was no English spoken, and I got along perfectly on my own, linking up with the director and the crew when and where necessary.

The Carlton Hotel on the Croisette overlooking the beach was the central meeting place for the film festival elite, and the lobby was jam-packed with everyone who wanted to see and be seen. Robert Redford was in Cannes, staying at the Carlton and sunning his golden-ness on the verandah to the admiration of people walking past on the pavement below. Alfred Hitchcock was honoured on the festival's final night.

I was so busy I had no time to see films, though I remember making a special effort to see the film all London's hippies were raving about: the wonderful animated cartoon of the *Fritz the Cat* underground comic books by Ralph Bakshi, who epitomized our pot-smoking, *Easy Rider* subculture. It was a great occasion, full of humour and good feelings. I wish I could have seen more films, for indeed it seemed that films were only seen by the local population, except for the galas at night which were social occasions for which tickets were very scarce.

Everyone was in Cannes to do business. Daytime hours were mostly spent in trying to make business deals and socializing.

People sat in cafes which lined the Croisette, the main seafront promenade avenue, and talked or showed off their tans, their name-brand accessories, their jewellery, their clothes, their faces.

There was also a great deal of sexuality in the air, fanned by starlets displaying their ample charms on the famous Cannes beach, which was merely a narrow stretch of gravel onto which fresh sand was trucked each morning and laid at the base of some stiff, small palm trees.

The Carlton bar was a maze of game-playing, where it seemed that every man was on the make and every woman fair game. I trod my way gingerly through this eye-opening flotsam and jetsam, as I arranged meetings and filming appointments with the various characters taking part in the film.

The *Savages* team had brought with them some elegant emerald-green and white, long-sleeved jerseys as giveaways, and they were much-sought-after status symbols among stars and near-stars that Cannes, as *Savages* was already the most talked-about film at the festival. I was glad to get one, and wear it. The director frowned when he saw me in it. I didn't care.

The arrival of film mogul Samuel Z. Arkoff and wife at Nice Airport was beautifully stage-managed for our cameras, with Arkoff pretending surprise at being greeted by a BBC film crew, though we knew he had certainly been informed in advance. Chomping on a fat cigar, he drove off to his suite at the extremely exclusive and expensive Hotel du Cap, a beautiful cliffside hotel situated in gardens of jasmine some distance down the coast from Nice.

We filmed the two English film-makers setting off in pursuit of a sale for their film, without which the success story already scripted by the director would not be complete. They had a very, very long search, finally persuading an Australian buyer, in the last moments before the film crew departed, to act out the presentation of a contract.

As our underground film director, he had rejected my selections and chosen instead a pretty blonde girl director of a really crazy underground film which seemed to have been filmed when everyone involved was on a separate psychedelic trip. I think it lasted for four hours, of which I had seen perhaps ten minutes. No one could say what it was about, especially not the blonde director, who was pretty and helpless-looking in her hipster pants, bikini top and belly button.

Working with such a man was not nice. He had a pasha-like behaviour and had convinced himself that he was making the film of all time. Like others before him and since, he believed he could depict reality by creating it, and he was busy trying to manufacture reality to his specifications, while ignoring the more interesting reality around him.

At the same time he felt uncomfortable around me, and was constantly challenging my Black attitude, trying to tear down the Black cushion behind which I tried to protect myself from falling back into the world from which I was successfully dragging myself. He resented this effort. But the falseness of the world we were in, not to mention the one he was creating, was precisely what I wanted to remove myself from.

Savages sent a beautifully designed, art nouveau brooch spelling the film's name in diamanté crystals to a most select set of people invited to the film's premiere. It was a hot ticket in the town and in a town of status symbols the brooch topped the demand for the jerseys. Still the director would not include *Savages* and Merchant-Ivory in the BBC film.

The premiere was packed with the very top people of the 1972 Cannes Film Festival, a Cannes celebrity event. The film was as elegant as a lace handkerchief and just as complex, but certainly an experience that merited discussion until final comprehension. Merchant-Ivory Films would not make much money, but would earn a lot of high-class artistic praise and respect. In years to come, as they have built their deserved and enormous reputation, *Savages* can be seen as the film which took them out of India and into mainstream American film-making.

The director would not film them. He could not even consider my invitation that he and the crew, without even carrying the film cameras, should come to the *Savages* after-premiere party. All alone with an old French taxi driver who spoke no English, I drove through the night across the French countryside, through the flower fields to Grasse and the elegant villa that housed the most elegant party thrown that season in Cannes.

Three other film crews covered the mass of richly dressed and famous guests circulating the torch-lit grounds of the villa, whose view stretched for miles to Cannes below. They feasted on Indian delicacies prepared by four chefs flown in from the best Indian restaurant in London, and they drank wine and champagne all night. It was a really good party.

Obviously, it was because they were MY friends, had been MY suggestion, that the director chose to leave out from his film such an important part of what Cannes 1972 had been. Maybe he just hadn't believed that anything that involved a Jamaican and an Indian could be worth anything. Certainly, when the film mogul mentioned next day, at a luncheon of lobster and champagne that he threw to impress us at the exclusive Hotel du Cap, that he was surprised that the BBC hadn't been there, the director did let slip a look of surprise.

I don't know how the lunchtime conversation turned to the subject of race, but I guess it always did in certain company when a Black person like me was present. This time it was the usual game of proving the Black race inferior. The mogul's wife was making some justification of Black inferiority on the basis of the number of Blacks who ruined their lives with drug addiction in New York's ghettoes.

Suddenly, I was tired of it all. I knew we weren't inferior. In fact, just looking around me at Cannes, this sick, money-oriented world, I could see that I was just about the only nice person in it. And I was nice BECAUSE I was Black, and it was my Blackness . . . my lack of guilt for the sins that I saw around me . . . the lack of my race's guilt for the creation of a world in which these sicknesses were highlighted as things to be praised . . . that made me a nice person.

I was not impressed by their wealth displayed around me, for I had experienced it all so many times before, so I was not in awe of them or it. My Blackness gave me the one thing which they each wished they had: beauty, dammit. Black WAS beautiful, in a way that White could never be.

Choosing my words carefully, and conscious that I was speaking on behalf of my race, I told her that Blacks would not be drug addicts if it were not part of a programme carried forward by White America to exterminate the race completely.

The film mogul choked on his cigar.

His wife spluttered.

I excused myself from their laden table.

For myself, I remembered a beach where the fine blonde powdery sand stretched for seventy times the length of the narrow strip of Cannes Croisette, where there was a small offshore island covered in tropical jungle that I could swim to across turquoise water, a beach and island that were only fifteen minutes' walk from my father's house in Port Antonio, Jamaica.

I took a taxi back to Cannes, packed my bag and booked a flight immediately back to London. I felt free, as if I had finally exited their world, shed the final skin.

Their false world was falsely real for them.

They were welcome to it.

Goodbye BBC.

Goodbye haters of all kinds.

Goodbye to pretending to be less important.

The farce was over.

The plane departed from Nice in a great rainstorm, taking me back to the comfort of my sweet man. He had stayed in my flat while I was away, and greeted me at the door.

'Your spirit was here all the time,' he said, as he welcomed me home with love.

I looked among my old Tourist Board papers and found a photo of that beach and that island, and pinned it up on the wall in front of my desk back at the *Man Alive* office. Suddenly, I knew that I wanted to be there more than anywhere else in the world.

And I was going to be there, too.

Soon.

The Prodigal would return.

Letting it be known that I did not wish my name to appear in the credits of the film, I stayed away from the editing room, sat at my desk and thought about Jamaica.

God was definitely on my side. One afternoon as I sat alone in the office, I got a phone call from Chris Blackwell at Island Records, whom I hadn't seen or spoken to for many years. He said he and Perry Henzell had made a film in Jamaica and they heard I had been at Cannes. They wanted me to promote the film for them, saying that I would need to fly down to Jamaica for the premiere in June, if I accepted.

I could only yell inwardly: 'Jamaica! For free!'

I contained myself enough to accept Chris's offer to come and view the film at Island's offices. Of course I accepted. No matter what the film was like, I would take the assignment. My dream was coming true and I could hardly contain my happiness.

There are times when I am forced to consider what a lucky person I am, and how much God loves me to have filled my life with so many beautiful experiences. As if in reward for cutting off my 'White hair', God gave me a beautiful Black man with whom I could be a Black woman. And as if in reward for rejecting Cannes and the Babylon world it represented, He gave me *The Harder They Come* and Jamaica in June.

The film was wonderful, a magical story which showed for the first time the Jamaica that exists beyond the white sand beaches of tourism. The most wonderful thing about it was that it was the first ever, and most realistic window into the Rastafari religion, culture and music. It was a watershed which showed the unique identity of Jamaica, and established reggae as a worldwide music.

As the film progressed and I saw my country and people with new eyes, I realized this was my life-raft back home. There was no turning back. Here was a most glorious reason to return to Jamaica. The new Jamaica of Michael Manley, of Rastafari, of Reggae, a Jamaica steeped in Black Power like raisins in wine for a rich wedding cake.

There have been few moments in my life more important or more far-reaching than the ninety minutes I spent watching *The Harder They Come* for the first time. In all, I have now seen it thirty-three times over the three decades since it was made, and each viewing repeats the emotions of joy and national passion which I felt on the first occasion.

Looking at the growing beauty of my new, natural hairstyle, I wondered why I had been depriving myself for so long of my greatest beauty asset, my hair. I shake my head in laughing self-mockery at the ridiculousness of it all. Hair, for Black women the wonderfully unique symbol of our Blackness, the mark of our beauty that sets us apart.

In the days of Cleopatra and Sheba and Tutankhamun's wife, we oiled and plaited it in thin braids decorated with gold, braids so fine as only our fine wool could retain braids neatly.

Our hair, which we had been taught to be afraid of, holding it stiffly out of all experiences, dreading a drop of rain or too much sweat, unable to swim or let the breeze blow through, or fingers caress, so as to retain its falseness in a silly attempt to pretend it was floppy and shiny like European hair.

How I wish I could personally tell every little Black girl to love her hair, to wash it every week, to condition it with oiling and brushing until it shines, to wind it in twists or plaits to keep it smooth, to fuzz it out wildly for fun or cover in modesty.

It's the Black woman's greatest trip, her hair. How she deals with it reflects the way she looks at life, you can be sure. It sends a woman's most powerful message. So you check the message she is sending when she covers her head with a White hairstyle.

Oh, I know there are lots of guys who like that White hairstyle. Maybe because it is the closest they can get to their heart's desire — a real White woman. But I'm only concerned with REAL Black men, the gods who are the very sweetest, the ones that only want a real Black woman. If that is the type that turns you on, an honest, good, upright, provider, handsome and sexy, well, I think I can say that the gods I have met are not turned on by imitation White hair.

And aren't you trying for a god?

Aren't you trying for the perfect specimen who would ensure your immortality, as well as your heaven on earth?

You aren't?

Yes, you are.

And deep in all Black men, aren't you aware of the god possibilities of your Blackness? Yes, or you wouldn't be so arrogant, wouldn't have survived the White man's attempt through slavery and racism to kill off your manhood.

So let's confess we are all dealing with the same desires, some more openly than others.

So why are we still fighting each other? Killing Black sisters and brothers every day, instead of reaching up and strangling the monster that fights to keep us from control of our Kingdom Africa, the seat of our Black Power?

Inferiority, the name of the White man's game.

Supremacy over Africa by the African at home and abroad, the name of Garvey's game.

On my way to act as a jury member at the Leipzig Film Festival, I stopped over in London in 1978 for the first time since leaving in December 1972, and went to Lorna St Clair for a wash and set. She laughed at the possibility, on seeing my thick wet locks of now long hair. But combed out and set on the biggest rollers, my hair came out from the dryer as straight as when she had been straightening it, bouncy and shiny and shoulder length. Lorna made me laugh, when she observed my beautiful smooth hair and wryly said: 'Don't come back . . . you'll lose me business!'

Yes . . . just ordinary nigger hair . . . tangled up at boarding school . . . full of salt water at holiday time . . . hidden in shame from birth . . . fried with heat and oil . . . assaulted by burning chemicals . . . now oiled and groomed and cared for to its fullest beauty. It needed no artificial agents to make it even more beautiful than the much-sought-after White straightness.

My gamble had paid off.

Chapter Fourteen

The Harder They Come was a most beautiful re-introduction to my lovely home, Jamaica. As I sat in the small screening room with a group of long-haired White Island staffers, I could hardly believe that Jamaica had produced a film like this, so realistic in its portrayal of the life of people at the bottom of the Jamaican social ladder; the world that the Tourist Board pretended did not exist. It was an unusual experience, that first viewing of *The Harder They Come*, which became the world's door into Jamaican culture.

The story with its Western-style hero, Ivan, modelled after a famous Jamaican outlaw 'Rhygin', was well told and excellently acted by Jamaicans, many of whom I knew. The music was vibrant, even though I couldn't understand the words of many of the songs.

Most intriguing of all was the fact that the film had been made by two White Jamaicans. I had first met Chris Blackwell when I was fifteen and he was a friend of my boarding-school friend Sally, the same Sally who was my friend in my first London days before she returned to Jamaica.

In fact, she had gone back to Jamaica and married Perry Henzell, the film-maker who employed Beverley Anderson, who invited me to be an extra on *A High Wind in Jamaica*, the film that brought me to England. That only goes to show how small Jamaican circles were, but for once this was a plus.

I was flown back to Jamaica to help prepare for the premiere, which coincidentally took place on my birthday. The premiere was a near riot in Kingston, as seemingly the entire population of the island tried to get into the cinema to see the film which was to become the most-loved film in Jamaica. It epitomized the mood of Jamaica at that time, the feeling that we were on the brink of a new age when righteousness would cover the earth through the Black vision of Rastafari, Socialism and non-racism.

Two White Jamaicans had made a powerful message for Black people, and Jamaicans were proud that it was their country that had done something so positive.

Clutching the VIP seating plan, I did not make it through the crush of people outside the cinema, and had to content myself with standing outside in the thick crowd listening to the roars of laughter and pleasure coming from inside the cinema. After the premiere party, which still stands out in my memory as the best party I have ever been to in my life, I returned to London determined to get back home as soon as possible.

First, I had to promote the film in England. I made up postcard invitations featuring the film's poster of Jimmy Cliff posing badman-style with two guns, and sent them out to fifty media and film journalists. On the day of the press screening, however, only two journalists turned up. One of them was my girlfriend Celia

Brayfield, then a *Daily Mail* reporter now a bestselling author. Apparently, I had timed the screening for the same hour as the screening for Marlon Brando's newest film *Last Tango in Paris*. I was crushed.

On Sunday morning, all the film review newspaper columns began with a comment on *Last Tango*. But the other journalist who had come to our screening happened to be the reviewer from the *Observer*, the most prestigious of the Sunday papers. He began his column with the words: 'Far and away the best film of the week is Jamaica's first feature film, *The Harder They Come*.'

It was enough. I was inundated with requests from sheepish film critics wanting to see the film. I arranged interviews for Jimmy Cliff, the film's star, with leading London newspapers and TV stations, while the film's theme song 'You Can Get It If You Really Want' entered the Top 40. It was a great time to be Black, Jamaican and in London.

The film opened in Brixton and ran to full houses, and the great delight of Jamaicans and West Indians all over London. Jamaicans laughed their heads off throughout scenes which British viewers saw as horrific depictions of ghetto life and violence. It was a film which opened their eyes to life outside their world, and they were astonished.

We took the film to the Film Festival at Cork, Ireland, and sat in the packed cinema where we Jamaicans were the only ones laughing. The hushed silence frightened us, but after the screening Perry Henzell and our team were greeted as heroes by the Irish and the film won an award for Best Editing.

Island Records flew me to Venice, the city where streets are water, for the Biennale Film Festival. I stayed at the famous Gritti Palace Hotel on the Grand Canal in the suite where Elizabeth Taylor had once stayed. On my first night there, while I waited for Perry and the others to arrive from Jamaica, I ordered dinner in my room and experienced the most fabulous room service ever, sitting beside a window overlooking the canal activity.

Venice was a most fascinating place, as you can imagine. It was incredible for a wide-eyed Jamaican girl to believe it was really me travelling in a gondola on the canals to the festival site. There was also time to walk through the narrow alleyways of Venice's ancient history, to stand in the famous Piazza San Marco and pose for photos with the pigeons. We visited the Venetian island famous for its blown glass, and watched the craftsmen fashion glassware in centuries-old traditions.

The Harder They Come won an award for Best Film Soundtrack at Venice, which pleased Blackwell enormously, though he and Perry later admitted they had mistaken the Venice Film Festival for Cannes when they had entered the film.

Being associated with the film was a wonderful and soulfully refreshing experience. When we returned, distributors from Britain's film industry made appointments with Chris Blackwell to discuss deals, none of which materialized for one reason or other, mostly to do with how unaccustomed distributors were to films by and about Black topics for Black audiences.

While I attended to my responsibilities for the film, I packed and prepared to leave England. I tumbled through a series of winding-down experiences in this period of trying to be with

Black people only, that sometimes found me in the company of a weird set of London Blacks on the edges of films and acting.

There was film star Calvin Lockhart, a very good-looking Black man from the Bahamas, whose rise to stardom had included the lead role in the hit British Swinging Sixties' film *Joanna*, and also a part in *Myra Breckinridge*, the famous film starring Raquel Welch and Mae West. One of the first Black British celebrities, he was given to much eccentric and boisterous show-off behaviour, and liked to travel in the company of his many outrageously odd Black friends. Lockhart persuaded me to accompany him to a 'film festival in Copenhagen' by telling me that my girlfriend Vonetta had asked me to meet her there and was expecting me.

He created a noisy scene at the airport, which got us both First Class seats and champagne on the plane, but when he created another scene at the hotel's front desk, unsuccessfully demanding to be given the Presidential Suite, then another scene outside the Presidential Suite itself in which Ike and Tina Turner were staying, I realized that I had better get away from that crazy man before he inflicted some damage on me personally. So while he went downstairs to negotiate his accommodation again, I slipped away and caught the first plane back to London.

Calvin's friends included a beautiful Trinidadian girl who shocked me by looking me straight in the eyes, smiling and informing me that she preferred girls. This was after I had spent several evenings in her company at her flat, which is where I had met Christine Keeler. Keeler, a sad shadow of her former beauty and charm, was in mad pursuit of Alfred Fagon, a muscled

Jamaican former postman, who was acquiring fame as a writer of accurate and humorous plays depicting the Black English scene.

The whole scene revolved in a small circle which included wealthy upper-class outsiders, handsome Black pimps, bejewelled Black madams who specialized in lesbian prostitutes and actual prostitutes who maintained apartments in the most fashionable areas. There were aspiring actors, film-makers, models, musicians and, of course, me.

I looked at the whole scene and realized that I had no business whatever in it, that it was just one more reason why I should get out of England as fast as I could to escape the gathering gloom of decadence, before I would fall into the trap and never, ever be able to extricate myself from its sticky entanglements.

I also found myself sadly having to accept that my Black man preferred White girls, since he returned to the rich White woman whom he had been living with when he met me. Maybe he hadn't yet met a Black woman who lived up to his ideal, and I was certainly new at the game.

But I remember a wonderful night when, feeling powerful in my Black beauty, dressed in a sleek beige jumpsuit with my hair newly released from small rollers to reveal a shiny crop of natural curls, I achieved the self-confidence to endure and prevail at an emotion-filled party where both he and his White woman were present. She was plump (no, tell the truth, fat and unattractive) and I felt no hatred of him or envy of her. I received too much admiration that night from other men, especially another handsome and good Black man who fell in love with me that night, though deep down I still loved that sweet man.

He drove me to the airport that December morning, where my friend Sonia, her husband and children – my god-daughters – waited to say goodbye to me.

I remember one particular memory of my last weeks which took me back to a weekend I had spent touring Paris with my Black American girlfriend. We were window-shopping along the wealthiest street in the world, the Rue du Faubourg Saint-Honoré, home of the famous fashion salons and such super-expensive shops as Gucci and Hermès.

In the Hermès window, I saw a most exquisite bed rug made up of patchwork squares of the softest vicuña wool. As I gazed at it, longing to touch its obvious softness, I thought to myself: 'That's what wealth is. To be able to have enough money to purchase that rug and have the privilege to touch its downy softness every day.'

Some weeks later, John Pringle asked me over for a drink, and there in his flat was the identical rug. I touched it and stroked it, and then it finally occurred to me that my previous view that one had to be rich to experience the best was not true in my case. My friend was rich and he had purchased the privilege. I had not a penny, but I was having as much pleasure for free as he was having by paying for it.

For me, the best things in life were free. I had always had them, never paid for them, because I had never wanted more than I had been given and had not pursued material goals. So I would always be richer by being able to appreciate the simple riches of just living life.

I had gotten Jamaica, Cannes, Europe, England, fine food, happy experiences . . . while some who had pursued the fullness of materialism had been reduced to failure and despair.

At my farewell party, the young Englishman who threw the party for me got frightened that cops might break in and find us smoking pot, with Christine Keeler wandering around looking for her mink coat. A friend from my White-only days, he panicked at being in the company of so many Black people at one time, and once again I was forced to consider how false had been some of the 'friendships' I had once so joyously entertained in England.

'Why are you leaving?' one friend asked me.

But another White girlfriend, Bill Oddie's wife Jean standing beside me, smiled and said: 'I know why.'

She did.

The week before I left, Vonetta had phoned anxiously, asking me to come to Africa with her. She was going to make a *Shaft* film there with Richard Roundtree, and wanted me as her companion.

No, I could not, would not detour or delay.

I was headed to my Zion.

I wanted to be in Jamaica, to see Rastafari, and to read my Bible.

I didn't realize that the detour she offered was Ethiopia, nor did I then realize the significance that country would come to have for me.

Yes, she met Emperor Haile Selassie I. She says his little dog jumped into her lap, the dog Rastas say was a lion.

Vonetta still teases me for not coming with her to Ethiopia.

One evening, after I had come home from showing *The Harder They Come* to Cubby Broccoli, producer of the James Bond films, in the private cinema in his luxury Knightsbridge home, I put the soundtrack album on the turntable for the umpteenth time. Suddenly as I looked at myself in the mirror, the beat of the music of Toots and the Maytals' 'Pressure Drop' got into me and, for the first time, I suddenly understood it, could feel the important rhythmic pattern, could dance with the proper movement to it and the rhythm of its words.

In that moment of exquisite liberation, I suddenly saw the beauty of my own face for the first time, saw its gentle rounded corners of eyes, and the triple petals of fleshy nostrils, the honey-brown skin shining with health, and the dark brown lips that were near plum in colour – all framed softly by the gentle lines of bubbly black hair.

It was a sobering sight, leading to a gentle smile of pleasure.

Yes, I WAS beautiful to look at.

Yes, Black WAS beautiful.

My hair, free from its binding prison of flat straightness, was now free to caress my Black features gently as nature intended, with a hairstyle for Black features instead of White styles for White features.

I wanted to hug Toots and the Maytals, and Jimmy Cliff and Ras Daniel Heartman, and everything about the film which had given me such a great present. I was truly free now, and all my new-found Black power gave me a potential for greatness which was unlimited.

So I came, I saw, I conquered. Without a clue as to the formula, nor even aware that it was happening, I became for a while the highest achieving Jamaican female in England in a serious field of journalism.

On the way I gained an enormous education in the various areas of my professional medium, including on-the-job lessons in television at the world's best school: British TV. I had lived in what is perhaps the world's most cosmopolitan city as a native and moved at ease in several of its most important circles, not least of which were the multi-faceted world of the Black immigrant, the media world and the social world.

And I had come to know myself well enough to discern that my race, far from being something to be treated as either a handicap or something one should pretend not to notice, was a beautiful strong tool that should be used for individual awareness by each member of our race. That knowledge was the tool that enabled me to conquer the feeling that I had in any way failed to achieve maximum, for by knowing the whole truth of our Black history, I could realize that only by assimilation into the ways and thinking of the White host race could I have achieved on its terms, in negation of my own.

The racial hatred I encountered made me replace a feeling of inferiority with self-confidence. Rather than stay and bow to it, I chose instead to gamble on the dream of Marcus Garvey that the reawakening of the power of my race is inevitable and occurring at this very moment, and that I can help to bring it about in some way by making a contribution of some sort in my own Black country to make it a bridge to Africa for those of us who wish to assist in Africa's restoration.

The gamble has paid off in many ways, not least of which has been peace of mind. As my hair continues to grow out, it appears to me like a reward, an assurance that I am doing the right thing, for believe it or not, it just gets prettier each day – much prettier than it was when it was straightened.

Some nice memories . . .

The music . . . Richie Havens . . . Bob Dylan . . . Jimi Hendrix . . . Taj Mahal . . . Roberta Flack . . . Boz Scaggs . . . Dory Previn's lament for single women . . . Carole King's *Tapestry* album . . . Janis Joplin . . . The Beatles . . .

The foods . . . mushrooms sautéed in butter . . . asparagus . . . avocado with prawns . . . veal scallopini . . . hummus and falafel . . . chicken dhansak . . . Portobello Road patties . . .

The places . . . Oxford Street at Christmas . . . cinemas in the afternoons . . . Indian restaurants . . . Greek restaurants . . . Habitat furniture . . . Biba dresses . . . the Number 7 bus route . . . Selfridges food store . . . Bond Street . . . Knightsbridge . . . Lee Ho Fook . . . Mr Chow . . . The Great American Disaster restaurant . . . the Roundhouse . . . discos and happenings . . . colour television . . . country-house weekends . . . good white wine.

And the people . . . Adrian and May Bailey . . . Carol Martin-Sperry . . . David Boardman . . . David Tong . . . David Lederman . . . Martin Robertson . . . Marian and Tessa Topolski . . .

Tricia and George . . . Pauline . . . Celia Brayfield . . . John who played tennis . . . Mike who ran . . . Richard who played . . . and Daniel who rowed . . .

. . . snow

. . . summer

. . . spring daffodils

. . . Montpelier Square

. . . England in the sixties.

. . . And one very special stoned Saturday afternoon in the mirrors and white walls of the Chow Two restaurant . . .

I said my farewell to England. England, you could keep the world that you didn't want to share. I had a bigger, better world to inhabit. I had my home: Jamaica. It was time for the prodigal to return.

Epilogue

I am a bad girl. Yes.

I am not a 'good' girl.

A 'good' girl would have come back from England and found herself a nice husband, someone with brown skin and 'good' hair (to keep the colour she inherited from her almost-White mother and straighten the children's noses), joined one of the Service Clubs – Rotary or Optimists or Friends of the British High Commission, or whatever – and settled into Jamaica's middle and upper social classes . . .

A 'good' girl would have taken her father's advice and looked pleased that his old friend, that old senior civil servant with a title from the Queen, Sir Somebody or Other, was interested in marrying a pretty young girl who would look after him patiently in his old age so she could inherit the house, the land and his wealth when he goes, and maybe have enough time left to catch a second husband before her looks were completely gone . . .

Or, a 'good' girl would have found herself a 'good' job, with some prestige and room for upward mobility, with a car and enough of a salary to merit a mortgage for a house, or an apartment – one of those town houses going up in New Kingston or Barbican or even Cherry Gardens – no time for husband and children, but lots of high-profile charity work . . .

Yes, a 'good' girl would have done so many things.

But I am not a good girl.

I do not accept the normal.

I came back home to Jamaica in 1972 and rejected the normal.

I made a firm decision to accept no society-constructed barriers to my accumulation of knowledge and experience, but to freely explore the new world of Jamaica into which I had entered after a decade in Britain – the country my education and upbringing had trained me to enter, but which I had not found a comfortable fit because of the attitude of the residents to my colour and country of origin, and despite my well-meaning but historically stupid reason for seeing England as my 'Mother Country'.

Oh no, I was seeking a complete contrast to all that. I wanted to be different, to begin my new life as a Jamaican, like a newborn babe, totally ignorant and uncaring of anything except the basics: eat, sleep, breathe, smile, be happy.

There were new roads to travel, new places to explore. Flowers to see, foods to eat, music to hear.

All of Jamaica to own as mine, my own, this lovely, beautiful place.

I wanted to walk barefoot on the beach at night again.

I wanted to play my guitar on a mountain balcony overlooking the city lights again.

I wanted to dive with the dolphins and swim with snapper fish again.

I wanted to spend a day in a river and bathe in its waterfalls again.

And I wanted to know who God is and if He knows that I exist.

I had a feeling that in Rastafari I could find the answer to that question.

I wanted, needed, to know more about Rastafari. It was a logical next stop on a personal development journey that had begun with living the musical and cultural revolution of the Swinging Sixties that was centred in London, combining the Eastern philosophies of the hippies, the sexual freedom of the Women's Movement and, most especially, the Black political revolution in which people like Angela Davis, Huey Newton, Malcolm X and Kwame Ture were special heroes and influencers.

The Garveyist philosophy Rastafari taught was the next natural political development for me from the Panthers' 'Black is Beautiful' philosophy, and I needed to know more about a movement that was speaking and acting and thinking in this way in my own country.

So, the lifestyle choice I made, to know more about and, eventually, become Rastafari, made me a bad girl, by Jamaica's moral judges, the people who decided who was 'accepted' and who was rejected from their circles. Thank heavens I had already decided to avoid those circles completely. They hadn't changed in my ten years' absence, only grown older.

The life I had chosen was far more interesting and, as time would eventually prove, a way of life that fitted in completely with the Jamaica that was to bloom out of the reggae seventies. From the cultural enrichment of London's Swinging Sixties, I came home in 1972 at the birth of a musical and cultural movement that grows bigger and wider as years go by. Within days of my return to Jamaica, I met the man who shone the brightest of reggae's musical lights around the world – Bob Marley. A small assignment put him in my life and he, his friends, his life and his religion were to become the most important experiences and life lessons of this bad girl.

Standing on the verandah of my father's Port Antonio house, whose lawn faced the sea, with the sounds of waves crashing on the rocks beyond and the swish of breeze through the fir trees that bordered his yard, I was a prodigal returning home.

It was a home in which I was a total stranger.

I realized that even though I had lived the majority of my life in the country of my birth, I didn't really know it. Despite growing up as a child, then a teenager, then a young adult at the birth of Jamaica's Independence, I had an education that taught me more about England and Europe than Jamaica and Africa. I knew more about the Wars of the Roses and Shakespeare and the climate of the Lake District than I knew about the little island on which I was born. I had been well taught, well trained in the Black Englishwoman brainwashing course known as a 'good Jamaican high school education'. Hampton and Wolmer's girls' schools may take credit.

Coming from ten years of using that knowledge to earn a living in England, I was as uninformed about Jamaica as any foreigner would be. My accent gave me away as I walked through the streets of Port Antonio, my little country hometown. My total ignorance of how things worked, how to buy food in the market, how to take a multi-person taxi, how to do anything the 'Jamaican' way, made me stand out as different.

I was like a newborn baby: innocent. Like a tourist visiting for the first time. Having grown up accepting being part of a colour and race that was second-class in the world, learning to accept and even love that negative fact about myself, 'being Black' was something different and new. It was about recognizing that being Black was something to be proud of, something good – with a new history, a new knowledge and attitude to be learned.

I was a very new student in 1972.

So I decided to be my own kind of good girl, to be the new version of myself that I wanted to be, seeing and hearing and tasting and experiencing life through the red, gold and green spectacles of Rastafari.

The Harder They Come had been my introduction to Reggae and to Rastafari. I was amazed to see in the film a side of Jamaica I had never before known or experienced. The music of downtown, which I had not experienced under the social ban prohibiting 'well-brought-up' girls like me from listening or dancing to our own home-made sounds, had evolved into a beautiful cultural experience of sound and lifestyle. The reggae music culture was like a strange country that had developed in the years I had been away. Jamaica was a place I did not know. I was eager to know this new country.

So I returned to Jamaica with a burning zeal to find out more about Rasta. What it was, what it meant, whether it was to be believed, or even lived. I had to know more. The film had opened my deepest curiosity with the scene of the iconic Rastaman Ras Daniel Heartman rising up from the sea flashing his locks, a strange yet proud banner of a new alternative way of life that preached simplicity, morality and a belief in a new kind of God who was Black.

This was a mystery to be explored because it intrigued me, it captured my mind in the empty space where belief in a God had been stirred since birth at many different spiritual stopping places, but never filled.

How to find it? All around me were the middle-class people I knew and half-knew before I left Jamaica, a melting pot of colours and races firmly embedded in their elevated aspirations to live the cultural life left behind by the colonial masters – a life where Rasta culture was either something to be scorned or afraid of, except for those who would find places and spaces to hide and smoke ganja with Rastas around town, and around country.

That life was not for me.

In my life so far, especially the decade in England meeting and moving among celebrities of fashion, film, music, media and revolutionary politics, I had already experienced everything I was interested in knowing about. I had lived the authentic high-class life in Britain already, mixing with top people in the best of British society. My experience did not make me want more; much less to live its imitation in Jamaica in attitudes, ideas and culture. I had found nothing yet as interesting, as intellectually and spiritually worth knowing more about, as Rastafari.

The Jamaican men I was meeting in the circles I was expected to move in were all boring. Politics men were the topmost social level, even higher than money men, who were a close second and often-times at an equal level of boredom. They all only talked about politics. Or money. I couldn't find any of them attractive. They were just simply boring.

My girlfriend Beverley was now married to the biggest politics man of all, the much-loved Prime Minister Michael Manley. Bev did her best to envelop me into her political social circle, but the more I met and spoke with the politicians who ran the country, the less I could find of interest among them.

I was told that Michael had used Rasta reggae artists in his round-the-island pre-election publicity tour and that it gave people hope that he would implement some Rasta-minded changes when he won. He had promised ganja law reform and the people expected some echoes of Garveyism, Black Power and perhaps a little Rasta too when he came to power, but while Rasta-minded people dreamed optimistically of going back to Africa, Michael went to Cuba instead to visit Fidel Castro and that was the start of the end of his Democratic Socialist dream to change Jamaica.

Such a pity.

Michael Manley was the handsome, well-spoken, charismatic leader Jamaicans felt we deserved, a Third World political super-star among the new leaders of African countries that had recently gained independence from colonial masters, many of them with Cuba's help. When Michael spoke, making his points eloquently in a fiery manner that reminded all of Fidel Castro's revolutionary appeal, he inspired people to have hope his party could change Jamaica for the better. It sounded good coming from Michael.

But I didn't hear any of the Marxist-Leninists around him saying anything that inspired me. There were definitely no Black Panthers among them, no Fidel Castros, no Mandelas, no Garveys. Just some people who had read a German man's manifesto on how to organize the world without God, which they were trying to implement in Jamaica. Religion, they said he had said, was the opiate of the masses – whatever that meant.

I couldn't understand what Marxism-Leninism or Democratic Socialism were. No one could explain either in a practical way. There was no attempt to educate us in what these systems were. These were just words. If you didn't know what those words meant, you were just one of the uneducated, illiterate 'lumpenproletariat' not worth including among the highly important political personalities running the government and the country. You were just 'voters' and 'crowd' to populate political meetings.

Like being in a foreign country whose language I didn't speak, being around such people was truly boring.

I was more interested in the political potential of Rastafari's Afrocentric philosophy as a way to build the new Jamaica. But there was little instruction on how to get to know more about that philosophy.

So I struck out into the unknown.

I said to a Rastaman I met on the fringe of one of the political meetings, 'I want to become a Rasta.'

He looked at me to see if I was serious, then said, 'I will take you to the teachers.'

He drove me down to East Kingston, to Slip Dock Road off Windward Road, where he picked up a man with a saxophone who he introduced as Tommy McCook. Then he drove further east up to Wareika Hill, to the Glasspole Avenue home of Brother Dougie Mack, my first Rasta teacher, who was to become the foundation of my knowledge of the history and livity of Rastafari.

Two houses away was the home and studio of the great Rastafari drummer Count Ossie, where Sam Clayton would 'teach' African history over the drumbeats of the Mystic Revelation of Rastafari.

We sat on stools among some men sitting in the shade of a zinc shelter at the back of Brother Dougie's house. He built me a spliff and Tommy McCook took up his saxophone and began to blow some of the sweetest music I had ever heard. The men smiled and made happy noises, one picked up an empty cooking pot and began beating a rhythm on the bottom, two others began to sing in harmony.

Thereupon began the happiest days of my life. Here, with the dirt of Brother Dougie's yard under my expensive London shoes and the smoke of the wood fire mixing with the smoke of ganja spliffs and chillum pipes being puffed by strange-looking men sitting all around me, I began my growing up as a Rasta.

I was so happy; I was smiling and smiling and smiling. Being in that backyard, so far away from everything and anything I had ever experienced in my life before, was simply the most wonderful experience of my entire life. It was a re-birth, the start of a new life in a Jamaica I had never known before, never even knew existed.

I feel that I was truly born again right there in 1972, a completely new person, given a chance to live my life all over again. A door had opened into a new world, and I was so very glad to be entering it, like an explorer finding a new civilization on a new planet.

Growing out is a process I recommend from my own experience – from imitating White to becoming genuinely Black. We should all go through this process in order to become wholly restored from the degrading inferiority complex of slavery to the all-encompassing pride in the history and inheritance of Africa.

So I say grow out, My beautiful Black Brothers and Sisters! Grow out your rich, Black layers with pride, and keep growing out.

Let your beautiful Black hair be a sign that you are aware of the greatness of your race, your history, your culture and your future potential.

Show that you know that Black is truly Beautiful.

Grow out!